Marketing in Japan

M. Y. Yoshino
foreword by Patrick M. Boarman and Richard C. King

This study has been sponsored by the
Center for International Business,
Pepperdine University,
Los Angeles and Malibu, California
Dr. Patrick M.Boarman, Director of Research

The Praeger Special Studies program—utilizing the most modern and efficient book production techniques and a selective worldwide distribution network—makes available to the academic, government, and business communities significant, timely research in U.S. and international economic, social, and political development.

Marketing in Japan
A Management Guide

PRAEGER SPECIAL STUDIES IN INTERNATIONAL ECONOMICS AND DEVELOPMENT

Praeger Publishers   New York   Washington   London

Library of Congress Cataloging in Publication Data

Yoshino, Michael Y
    Marketing in Japan.

  (Praeger special studies in international economics and development)
    1. Marketing—Japan. I. Title.
[HF5415.12.J3Y69]   658.8'00952   74-3576
ISBN 0-275-09170-8

PRAEGER PUBLISHERS
111 Fourth Avenue, New York, N.Y. 10003, U.S.A.
5, Cromwell Place, London SW7 2JL, England

Published in the United States of America in 1975
by Praeger Publishers, Inc.

All rights reserved

© 1975 by Praeger Publishers, Inc.

Printed in the United States of America

FOREWORD
Patrick M. Boarman
and Richard C. King

In the wake of the extraordinary success of the Japanese in selling their wares to foreigners, especially to Americans, a pragmatic analysis of the characteristics of the Japanese marketplace is especially timely. The secular tendency for Japanese exports to outpace Japanese imports has tended to complicate Japan's relations with other countries, and especially the United States, to say the least. If this trend is not to continue indefinitely, it is vital that businessmen in Japan's major partner countries become aware of the special features of Japan's marketing and distribution system.

M. Y. Yoshino, Professor of Management at the Graduate School of Management, University of California at Los Angeles, and recently Visiting Professor at the Harvard School of Business Administration, is an acknowledged authority on the Japanese marketing system. In this book, intended primarily for businessmen interested in exploiting the Japanese market, but also for students of the Japanese economy generally, Professor Yoshino provides us with a series of profiles—geographic, demographic, economic, social, and managerial—of the Japanese marketing and distribution system, the lineaments of which are impressive enough:

— with an area less than that of California but a population five times as large (105 million), Japan has a population density exceeded by only a few other countries;
— its GNP is second only to that of the U.S. among democratic countries, having recently surpassed that of West Germany and the United Kingdom;
— the average annual real growth of the Japanese economy in the last 15 years has been 10%, versus 3.7% for the U.S., 4.7% for Germany, 5.7% for France, and 5.8% for Italy;
— benefits of growth have been widely diffused, making Japan the second largest mass market in the world;
— Japan is the most literate nation with a literacy rate of almost 100%; its consumers are also among the best educated;
— its mass media coverage is proportionately greater than anywhere else in the world, with 117 newspapers reaching 53 million persons, 2500 magazines, and 18,000 books produced annually.

Moreover, the vast potential of the market indicated by these numbers is increasing as a result of ongoing profound changes in the Japanese way of life. While the birth rate is declining, the extended family system is breaking down, giving rise to many new households. And though the high rate of savings—a Japanese characteristic reflecting the traditional asceticism of the people—continues as a factor of importance in the Japanese economy, a great consumer revolution—shohi kakumei—has been under way in recent years which holds important implications for consumption and for growth.

Even the problems that have arisen in the wake of Japanese economic growth have marketing implications. Environmental deterioration and the ensuing public concern over it have generated product needs of an entirely new kind in Japan. The deficient state of Japan's infrastructure—of its roads, sewage disposal systems, parks, etc., and the shortage of good housing—are obvious clues to future areas for market development.

Professor Yoshino is particularly knowledgeable about the famous Japanese trading companies—those unique institutions with no precise analogue anywhere else, which constitute such an important part of the Japanese distribution system. And his book includes a section on the trading companies which could stand on its own as a model of lucid exposition and analysis.

The Center for International Business of Pepperdine University is pleased to have sponsored this guide to the Japanese market as another in a series of publications aimed at enabling American businessmen to cope more effectively with the opportunities and the risks of the new international competition.

PREFACE

This book is designed to be a practical guide to businessmen interested in penetrating the Japanese market. Japan is the second-largest mass market in the world. Former iron-tight restrictions against foreign firms have been radically liberalized. Particularly, the last round of capital liberalization has removed virtually all the restrictions. Penetration of the Japanese market, however, is by no means easy and it is my hope that this book will be a useful guide. This book builds on my previous research on the Japanese marketing system, but substantial new materials have been added and important recent developments have been noted.

Many people have contributed to this study. I interviewed scores of businessmen, government officials, and others who are knowledgeable about the Japanese marketing system. They have generously contributed their time and information. Some of the interviews were undertaken by Mr. Jeffrey Lloyd of UCLA and Dr. K. Hayashi of the Japan Institute of International Business Studies. They performed their assignment excellently. Of course, I alone assume all responsibility for the study.

Mrs. Grace Marshall, a close associate and a dear friend, as usual performed many important tasks in completing this book. Mrs. Sheila Burnham patiently and willingly worked through my almost illegible handwriting. To her goes my sincere gratitude. Miss Sharon Outzen conscientiously typed the final manuscript.

This study was supported by the Center for International Business of Pepperdine University. I am very grateful to Mr. Richard King, Executive Director of the Center, who first encouraged me to undertake the study. Dr. Patrick Boarman, Research Director of the Center, has been most generous and understanding in providing his support. Without the patience and unflagging interest of these two outstanding men, this book would have never come into being.

CONTENTS

	Page
FOREWORD Patrick M. Boarman and Richard C. King	v
PREFACE	vii
LIST OF TABLES AND FIGURE	xi

Chapter

1	THE JAPANESE MARKET	1

    Geographic Considerations   2
    Demographic Profile   5
    Economic Profile   7
        Japan's Phenomenal Economic Growth   7
        The Emerging Mass Market   11
        Savings and Consumption Patterns   13
    Social Aspects   17
        Consumption Orientation   19
        Westernization   20
        Education and Mass Media   21
        Convenience Orientation   24
        Leisure Orientation   25
    Problems Facing Japanese Consumers   27
    The Rising Tide of Consumerism   29

2	THE JAPANESE DISTRIBUTION SYSTEM: AN OVERVIEW	31

    Growth of the Distribution System   32
    Distinctive Features of the Marketing System   32
        Fragmentation   32
        The Pivotal Position of Wholesalers   35
        The Many Levels of Distributors   36
        The Limited Number of Customers   36
        Wholesalers' Dependence on Credit   37
    Changes in the Wholesaling System   39
        The Failure of Many Wholesalers to Adapt   41
        Adaptive Behavior of Progressive
            Wholesalers   43
    The Retailing Sector   44

Chapter		Page
	Fragmentation	45
	How Retailers are Adapting to Change	46
3	LARGE-SCALE RETAIL ENTERPRISES	55
	Emergence of Mass Merchandising Firms	55
	Reasons for Rapid Growth	56
	Kinds of Products Sold	58
	The Entrepreneurs of Mass Merchandising	58
	Supermarket Chains	60
	Trend Toward Greater Concentration	61
	Diversity of Product Lines	62
	Financial Ratios	63
	Installment Credit Stores	65
	Specialty Chain Stores	65
	Traditional Marketing Institutions	66
	Implications and Future Prospects for Retailing	67
	The Power Struggle in Distribution	68
	Major Challenges	73
	New Strategies	79
4	OTHER RECENT MARKETING DEVELOPMENTS	83
	Marketing Innovations by Large Manufacturers of Consumer Goods	83
	Forces for Change	83
	Responses to Changing Conditions	85
	Evolution of a New Distribution System	85
	Price Maintenance	92
	Conclusion	93
	Growth of Self-Service	94
	The Role of Department Stores	97
	Threats to Traditional Department Stores	106
	Response to the Challenge	107
	Development of Shopping Centers	108
	Growth of Consumer Financing	110

Chapter		Page
5	JAPANESE TRADING COMPANIES	117
	Evolution	118
	Structure	120
	Functions	122
	Development of New Businesses	125
	The Sources of Trading Companies' Strength	128
	The Benefits of Group Affiliation	128
	International Information Network	129
	Excellence in Management	130
	Financial Services	130
	Financial Performance	132
	Entry into the Retail Sector	136
	Major Problems of Trading Companies	140
	Other Problems of Trading Companies	141
6	STRATEGY GUIDE TO THE JAPANESE MARKET	145
	Exporting to Japan	145
	How to Penetrate the Market	146
	How to Select a Distributor	148
	Joint Ventures	149
	How to Negotiate in Japan	152
	How to Deal with the Government	154
ABOUT THE AUTHOR		157

LIST OF TABLES AND FIGURE

Table		Page
1.1	Relative Importance of Consumer Markets in Japan by Region and Prefecture, 1971	3
1.2	Standards of Living for Japanese Households by Region and Prefecture, 1971	4
1.3	Projected Japanese Population by Age Categories for Selected Years, 1970-90	5
1.4	Number and Average Size of Japanese Households for Selected Years, 1945-70	7
1.5	Sectorial Distribution of the Japanese Labor Force, 1960-70	8
1.6	Change in the Type of Worker in the Japanese Labor Force, 1960-70	9
1.7	Wage Increases in Japan for Selected Years, 1955-70	9
1.8	Income Distribution in Japan, 1959, 1962, and 1968	10
1.9	Average Annual Income of Agricultural Households for Selected Years, 1955-70	11
1.10	Income Gains Reported by Five Income Classes in Japan, 1963-69	12
1.11	Japanese Ownership of Selected Consumer Durables, 1971	12
1.12	Household Expenditure Patterns of Nonagricultural Households in Cities with Population of 50,000 or More, 1956-68	14
1.13	Household Expenditure Patterns of Agricultural Households in Cities with Population of 50,000 or More, 1956-67	15

Table		Page
1.14	Indices of Expenditure Levels by Major Categories for Urban Nonagricultural Households, 1956-68	16
1.15	Indices of Expenditure Levels by Major Categories for Agricultural Households, 1956-67	17
1.16	Yearly Average of Monthly Disbursements for Living Expenditures per Household by Monthly Income Quintile Groups, 1968	18
1.17	Annual Expenditure for Selected Food Products in Japan for Selected Years, 1963-69	21
1.18	Japanese Expenditure for Selected Western-Style Furniture by Income Group, 1971. Nonagricultural and Agricultural	22
1.19	Growth of Total Advertising Expenditure in Japan, 1955-70	24
1.20	Distribution of Advertising Expenditure by Major Media, 1970	25
1.21	Leisure-Related Expenditure by Urban Households for Selected Years, 1965-70	26
2.1	Growth of Wholesale and Retail Sectors, 1952-68	33
2.2	Wholesale and Retail Establishments in Japan by Size, 1970	34
2.3	Number of Customers per Day, 1970	35
2.4	Types of Wholesaling Activities, 1970	37
2.5	Wholesale Establishments According to Customer Groups, 1970	38

Table		Page
2.6	Average Number of Customers by Wholesaler Size, 1970	39
2.7	Wholesalers' Methods of Payment for Purchases and Receipts for Sales by Size of Firm, 1970	40
2.8	Small Retailers' Evaluation of Services Provided by Wholesalers in Selected Areas, 1968	42
2.9	Relative Importance of Retail Outlets in Japan, 1970	45
2.10	Number of Retail Stores With and Without Paid Employees, 1958 and 1968	46
2.11	Size of Retail Establishments in Japan by Number of Employees, 1958-70	47
2.12	Size of Retail Establishments in Japan by Floor Space, 1962-67	48
2.13	Retail Stores by Category, 1970	49
2.14	Retail Sales by Type of Store, 1970	50
2.15	Annual Sales per Salesperson and per Square Meter of Sales Space, by Categories of Stores, 1970	51
2.16	Sales Space per Employee and Stock Turnover by Type of Store, 1970	52
3.1	Key Indicators of the 100 Largest Mass Merchandising Firms, 1971	57
3.2	Total Purchases Made at Supermarkets for Selected Food Products, 1971	58
3.3	Total Purchases Made at Supermarkets for Selected Nonfood Products, 1971	59

Table		Page
3.4	Estimated Total Sales of Selected Key Product Categories Sold by Mass Merchandising Firms and Department Stores, 1971	59
3.5	Concentration of Supermarket Sales Among the Large Firms, 1971	61
3.6	The Ten Largest Supermarket Chains in Japan Ranked by Sales, 1971	62
3.7	Major Merchandise Categories of Japanese Supermarket Chains, 1971	63
3.8	Average Key Financial Ratios of the 100 Largest Supermarket Chains, 1968 and 1971	64
3.9	Key Operating Ratios, Daiei Chain, 1971	64
3.10	Projected Retail Sales by Types of Stores, 1969-80	73
3.11	Actual and Projected Sales of Merchandise by Type of Retail Store, 1970 and 1975	74
4.1	Advertising Expenditures by Major Japanese Corporations, 1971	86
4.2	Number of Japanese Manufacturers Requiring Resale Price Maintenance for Selected Products, 1962-68	93
4.3	Growth of the Self-Service Concept in Japan, 1964-70	95
4.4	Distribution of Self-Service Stores by Size of Sales Space, 1968-70	97
4.5	Distribution of Employees and Sales in Self-Service Stores by Size of Store, 1966-70	98

Table		Page
4.6	Performance Data of Self-Service Stores by Size of Store, 1970	99
4.7	Total Sales of Department Stores, 1960-68	101
4.8	Growth of Department Store Sales, 1965-70	102
4.9	Financial and Operating Results of Selected Department Stores, 1968	103
4.10	Financial and Performance Characteristics of Department Stores in Japanese Cities of Various Sizes, 1970	104
4.11	Monthly Sales per Employee According to Number of Employees, 1970	105
4.12	Monthly Sales per Employee According to Size of Store, 1970	105
4.13	Installment Credit According to Income Classes, 1970	111
4.14	Percentage of Total Sales Through Installment Purchase of Selected Products, 1968	112
5.1	The Ten Largest Trading Companies, 1971	121
5.2	The Major Companies of Japan and the New Industries Each Plans to Enter	127
5.3	Return on Investment (Before Taxes) for Six-Month Term Ending March 1972	133
5.4	Selling, General, and Administrative Expenses of the Ten Leading Trading Companies as a Percentage of Sales Revenues, 1969-70	134

Figure

| 5.1 | Annual Growth Rate of the Ten Leading Trading Companies by Type of Commodities Handled, 1970 | 135 |

Marketing in Japan

CHAPTER

1

THE JAPANESE MARKET

In approaching any market, understanding its relevant characteristics is the first essential step. The Japanese market is no exception. In light of its very dynamic character, a thorough knowledge of the Japanese consumer market is essential to any American company interested in doing business with Japan. The Japanese market is an extremely attractive one. Second only to the United States, it is the largest mass market in the world. It is fast growing. Moreover, some rapid changes are taking place in consumer tastes and life style. The combination of these forces means that great opportunities exist for profit by imaginative American companies.

The rapidly emerging mass market in Japan is taking on many of the characteristics that are already commonplace in the United States. Thus, American experience, if discreetly applied, would provide our U.S. companies with significant advantages. It goes without saying, however, that the Japanese market is an extremely complex one. Dynamic growth and change are not unmixed blessings. Changes, unless their implications are well understood, can also mean pitfalls. Indeed, to a substantial number of American companies, entry into the Japanese market has proved to be a bitter and frustrating experience.

Moreover, the Japanese market is one of the most competitive in the world. Japanese consumers are becoming increasingly discriminating. They are becoming powerful in the marketplace and they are not loath to use their newly gained power. It is, therefore, no easy task to enter, let alone penetrate, the market. In a book designed for practical analysis of consumer practices and market opportunities, there is no better place to begin than with the examination of salient characteristics of the consumer market. After a brief geographical note this chapter will be devoted to the consideration of demographic, economic, and social characteristics of the rapidly growing consumer mass market.

GEOGRAPHIC CONSIDERATIONS

Knowledge of the location of attractive markets is essential to marketing planning. This is particularly important in the case of Japan for two reasons: (1) the very small size of the country is rather deceiving, and those uninitiated often are tempted to develop marketing programs without due regard to regional differences; (2) the relative attractiveness of certain regional markets within Japan is rapidly changing because of the increasing mobility of the population.

Let us now examine the relative attractiveness of various Japanese regional markets as they are today. Japan is divided into 46 political units known as prefectures. Considerable data are available on the prefectural level. We must recognize, of course, that statistics based on the political unit are not necessarily suitable for the purpose of marketing planning, but nevertheless they provide meaningful insights and can serve as a useful guide.

For this purpose, we shall draw from carefully calculated indices of relative purchasing power developed by the Oriental Economist. This particular purchasing-power index is constructed by giving equal weight to the following ten variables: population, bank deposits, postal savings, insurance ownership, retail sales, restaurant sales, income of theaters, beer consumption, ownership of passenger cars, and number of new homes constructed. No doubt such a generalized index has its own limitations and must be used with caution; it is nevertheless highly useful in providing an overall picture. Table 1.1 presents a breakdown for overall purchasing power. These data reveal very significant facts about the Japanese market for each region and prefecture. That is, nearly 30 percent of the purchasing power is concentrated in the southern (Minami) Kanto region, 19 percent in the Kinki region, and slightly over 10 percent in the Tokai region. This means that almost 60 percent of the purchasing power of the nation is concentrated in three highly industrialized urban regions.

Table 1.2 presents a comparison of standards of living on a household basis for all the regions and prefectures. The national average is indicated as 100. This index is calculated on a household basis by using all of the factors considered above with the exception of population. The data reveal considerable geographic differences in the standard of living. As might be expected, Tokyo leads all other prefectures by a substantial margin, followed by Osaka, Aichi, and Kyoto. By far the lowest is Kagoshima prefecture on Kyushu, whose index is less than a third of the Tokyo standard.

Japan is a small country with a total area less than the state of California; but, as evident from the foregoing consideration,

TABLE 1.1

Relative Importance of Consumer Markets in Japan
by Region and Prefecture, 1971
(national total = 100 percent)

Hokkaido	4.56		Kinki	19.02
			Shiga	0.76
Tohoku	6.44		Kyoto	2.47
Aomori		0.99	Osaka	9.68
Inate		0.90	Hyogo	4.45
Miyagi		1.43	Nara	0.72
Akita		0.90	Wakayama	0.94
Yamagata		0.90		
Fukushima		1.32	Sanin	0.98
			Tottori	0.44
Kita Kanto	4.11		Yammane	0.54
Ibaragi		1.53		
Tochigi		1.20	Sanyo	5.20
Gumma		1.38	Okayama	1.42
			Hiroshima	2.45
Minami Kanto	29.31		Yamaguchi	1.33
Saitama		2.88		
Chiba		2.74	Shikoku	3.13
Tokyo		18.23	Tokushima	0.60
Kanagawa		5.46	Kagawa	0.79
			Ehime	1.09
Hokuriku	4.40		Kochi	0.65
Niigata		1.87		
Toyama		0.89	Kitakyusun	7.25
Ishikana		0.95	Fukaoka	3.58
Fukui		0.69	Saga	0.59
			Nakasaki	1.10
Tozan	3.67		Kumamato	1.11
Yamanashi		0.56	Oita	0.87
Nagano		1.63		
Gifu		1.48	Minami Kyushu	1.70
			Miyazaki	0.73
Tokai	10.24		Kagoshima	0.97
Shizuoka		3.04		
Aiichi		5.89		
Mie		1.31		

Source: Economic Planning Agency.

TABLE 1.2

Standards of Living for Japanese Households by Region and Prefecture, 1971
(national total = 100)

Hokkaido	88.75		Kinki	117.60
			Shiga	92.64
Tohoku	78.71		Kyoto	110.84
Aomori		71.26	Osaka	130.29
Inate		68.26	Hyogo	100.99
Miyagi		85.62	Nara	83.41
Akita		78.63	Wakayama	90.14
Yamagata		81.62		
Fukushima		73.65	Sanin	75.92
			Tottori	78.91
Kita Kanto	86.86		Yammane	70.43
Ibaragi		80.41		
Tochigi		84.01	Sanyo	94.71
Gumma		92.23	Okayama	82.44
			Hiroshima	100.94
Minami Kanto	129.01		Yamaguchi	86.87
Saitama		82.03		
Chiba		90.68	Shikoku	81.17
Tokyo		151.19	Tokushima	76.85
Kanagawa		103.75	Kagawa	88.31
			Ehime	74.45
Hokuriku	97.42		Kochi	77.04
Niigata		87.84		
Toyama		96.72	Kitakyusun	81.54
Ishikana		102.12	Fukaoka	88.78
Fukui		105.37	Saga	74.77
			Nakasaki	69.24
Tozan	90.45		Kumamato	64.85
Yamanishi		78.09	Oita	74.69
Nagano		88.62		
Gifu		92.89	Minami Kyushu	56.75
			Miyazaki	65.32
Tokai	117.33		Kagoshima	48.77
Shizuoka		111.15		
Aiichi		121.50		
Mie		90.68		

Source: Economic Planning Agency.

attractive markets are highly concentrated and marketing efforts must be planned accordingly.

DEMOGRAPHIC PROFILE

Japan's population reached slightly over 103 million in 1971, which places Japan sixth in world population. For the past decade or so, the Japanese population has been growing about 1 percent annually. This rate is expected to continue through this decade, at which point the population is projected to be around 116 million. The percentage distribution by age to 1990 is presented in Table 1.3. After 1980 the growth rate is expected to decline substantially.

While Japan ranks sixth in world population, in terms of population density she ranks fourth, exceeded only by Belgium, the Netherlands, and Great Britain. In terms of population density per square foot of arable land, Japan leads all other nations. Not only is Japanese population density among the highest in the world, but the population is concentrated in certain areas. Honshu, the largest island, occupies 65 percent of the total area, but has nearly 80 percent of the population. Kyushu, with 11 percent of the total area, claims roughly 12 percent of the population. Most sparsely populated is the island of Hokkaido, which accounts for over 21 percent of the land area, but only 5 percent of the population. The smallest of the major islands, Shikoku, has slightly over 3 percent of the population.

TABLE 1.3

Projected Japanese Population by Age Categories
for Selected Years, 1970-90
(in thousands and percentages)

	Total	0-14	15-59	60 and over
1970	103,744	24,699	68,003	11,042
	(100)	(23.8)	(65.6)	(10.6)
1975	109,935	26,347	70,652	12,926
	(100)	(24.0)	(64.3)	(11.6)
1980	115,972	27,914	73,413	14,646
	(100)	(24.1)	(63.3)	(12.6)
1990	124,744	27,519	77,605	19,620
	(100)	(22.1)	(62.2)	(15.7)

Source: Economic Planning Agency.

Among the advanced nations, Japan has the highest percentage of productive population, that is, those between 15 and 65 years old. Almost 66 percent of the entire population falls into this category in comparison to 64.5 percent for West Germany and 61 percent for the United States. Persons who are 65 years old or over in Japan account for less than 7 percent of the population in contrast to 9.6 percent, 12.2 percent, and 12.8 percent for the United States, West Germany, and Great Britain, respectively. This segment, however, is rapidly growing in all these countries. At the same time, the segment of population younger than 15 years, which in 1950 accounted for 35 percent of the population, has been declining.

Then, the Japanese population is highly concentrated in major urban areas. As high as 72 percent of the nation's total population is found in land area of less than 25 percent. Metropolitan Tokyo alone claims over 10 percent of the population, and there are eight cities with one million or more in population. These cities are Tokyo, Osaka, Yokohama, Nagoya, Kyoto, Kobe, Kitakyushue, and Sapporo. These eight major cities account for slightly over 20 percent of the population. Most densely populated is the narrow coastal strip of land between Tokyo and Osaka.

The Japanese population has become increasingly mobile in recent years. Particularly notable has been the influx of large numbers of people to urban industrial areas. Between the censuses of 1965 and 1970, 26 prefectures recorded a large increase in the population, and among them were six that recorded over 10 percent growth in the five-year period. All of these six prefectures are found near the three major metropolitan areas, Tokyo, Osaka, and Nagoya. The continuing trend for concentration of the population has resulted in a considerable imbalance in its distribution, and has created some serious social problems.

A third significant development is the rapid increase in the number of families, and corresponding reduction in average family size. This can be seen in Table 1.4. Traditionally, the Japanese have been known for large families, and it was not uncommon to find two or three generations living together. Indeed, the Japanese have been known for a close and tightly knit family system. During the past two decades, however, the average family size has been steadily declining. The size of an average family in Japan is indicated by household size, which is now 3.7 persons. Between the censuses of 1955 and 1970, the number of households increased from 20.7 million to 27.8 million, a 34 percent increase.

Behind this trend are two significant forces. One is the declining birth rate. Even more significant is the breakdown of the traditional concept of an extended family, with several generations living together. This tradition is rapidly disappearing, particularly in major urban

TABLE 1.4

Number and Average Size of Japanese Households
for Selected Years, 1945-70
(in thousands and percentages)

Year	Nationwide		Urban		Rural	
1945	15,871	4.90	5,921	4.37	9,950	5.25
1955	20,656	4.76	13,779	4.86	6,876	4.56
1965	24,082	4.08	17,138	3.90	6,944	4.52
1970	27,757	3.72	20,864	3.58	6,893	4.16

Source: Economic Planning Agency.

areas. Indeed, the concept of family itself has been undergoing a significant change in Japan during the postwar decades. Nearly 57 percent of the families now are the so-called nuclear type, which consist of married couples with or without children. In only one out of five families do three generations or more live together as a family unit. This trend means that the number of new household formations has been increasing at a rapid rate which, of course, has important marketing implications.

ECONOMIC PROFILE

Having examined demographic aspects of the Japanese market, let us now turn our attention to an economic profile of Japanese consumers. The story of the phenomenal economic growth of Japan following World War II has been told many times, and certainly it need not be repeated here in detail. The main thrust of the discussion to follow is an examination of how such rapid economic growth has benefited average consumers, giving rise to the second largest mass market in the world. The following considerations are sufficient to demonstrate the nation's postwar economic growth.

Japan's Phenomenal Economic Growth

1. Japan's GNP, having surpassed that of England and West Germany in the late 1960s, now stands second only to that of the United States.

2. The average annual real growth of the Japanese economy during the past decade and a half has exceeded 10 percent. During the same period, the average growth rate of the GNP of other leading nations was 3.7 percent for the United States, 2.8 percent for Great Britain, 4.7 percent for West Germany, 5.7 percent for France, and 5.8 percent for Italy.

This rapid rate of economic growth has had a significant impact on the Japanese economy and society. For one thing, during the last decade or so the Japanese economy has been able to maintain full employment. The unemployment rate has been typically less than 1 percent. The rapid growth rate has also altered substantially the employment structure. As can be seen from Table 1.5, the labor force has shifted significantly from the primary to secondary and tertiary sectors. A rather significant increase in the relative number of wage earners in the labor force has also occurred. Now, over 65 percent of those who are gainfully employed are wage earners. Also significant is the marked decline of family workers, those who are "employed" in family businesses, as shown in Table 1.6.

One of the most significant aspects of the postwar economic growth is the fact that its benefits have been widely diffused. This is largely due to a series of dramatic reform measures undertaken in the immediate aftermath of the war. The single class that has benefited most are wage earners. Not only do wage earners as a class now account for over 65 percent of the labor force, they have experienced a steady increase in wages.

As can be seen in Table 1.7, in the manufacturing industry, for example, the wage level has almost doubled in real terms between 1960 and 1970. A recent government survey reveals that in 1970

TABLE 1.5

Sectorial Distribution of the Japanese
Labor Force, 1960-70
(in percentages)

	1960	1965	1970
Primary sector	30.2	23.5	17.5
Secondary sector	28.0	31.9	35.1
Tertiary sector	41.8	44.6	47.5
	100.0	100.0	100.0

Source: Ministry of Labor.

TABLE 1.6

Change in the Type of Worker in the Japanese
Labor Force, 1960-70
(in percentages)

	1960	1965	1970
Proprietors	22.7	19.9	19.2
Wage earners	53.4	60.8	65.0
Family workers	23.9	19.3	15.8
	100.0	100.0	100.0

Source: Ministry of Labor.

TABLE 1.7

Wage Increases in Japan for
Selected Years, 1955-70
(1965 = 100)

Year	All Industries	Manufacturing
1955	67.8	67.1
1960	82.6	83.5
1965	100.0	100.0
1970	146.1	152.4

Source: Ministry of Labor.

the average income of wage earners' households increased to ¥1,170,000.* Per capita annual income now stands at around $1,800. Although this is still less than half of the United States' level, it is greater than that of Great Britain and is rapidly approaching that of West Germany.

Another impressive evidence of marked improvement in the income level during the past decade can be seen from Table 1.8. In 1959 over 90 percent of the households had an annual income of less

---

*At the time of writing, 1971, ¥360 equalled 1 U.S. dollar.

TABLE 1.8

Income Distribution in Japan, 1959, 1962, and 1968

Income (in ¥)	1959	1962	1968
Less than 600,000	20,740	19,447	12,127
600,000-999,999	1,418	3,329	8,684
1 million-1,499,999	396	852	4,730
1.5 million-1,999,999	–	404	1,693
2 million and over	–	–	1,285
Total	22,554	24,032	28,519

Source: Kokumin Seikatsu Hakusho, 1971, p. 341.

than ¥600,000. A decade later this segment declined to less than 43 percent. Over 27 percent had an annual income of at least ¥1 million. Nearly 5 percent of the Japanese households had an income of at least ¥2 million in 1968.

The combination of the relative increase in the number of wage earners and the steady wage level increase has contributed to a shift in the shares going to various income recipients. Wage earners now claim nearly 55 percent of the national income. The share of the national income going to individual proprietors is now around 22 percent. The combination of wartime destruction and dislocation, postwar inflation and Occupation reforms has all but wiped out the traditional rentier class in Japan, which class as a whole now claims slightly over 10 percent of national income.

Along with wage earners, farmers too have made substantial relative gains. Here several developments are noteworthy. First, the Occupation-sponsored agricultural reforms changed the pattern of land ownership in Japan. In 1941, for example, less than a third of agricultural households owned completely the land they cultivated, whereas at present over 80 percent of farmers do so. Pure tenant farmers now are less than 2 percent of the total farm population.

Second, while the Japanese agricultural sector still has much room for modernization, this sector has gained a substantial increase in productivity. The third significant aspect is that four out of every five agricultural families have income from nonagricultural sources. In fact, in over 40 percent of the households, the income obtained from sources other than farming exceeds that received from farming. In the aggregate, over half of the income claimed by agricultural households is obtained from nonfarming activities. The combination of these factors with the price support for rice and the high prices commanded by agricultural products have brought unparalleled prosperity to agricultural households. As evident from Table 1.9, in 1970 the average income of agricultural households reached almost ¥1.4 million. One of the most significant aspects of Japan's postwar economic development is that the two most deprived segments in the prewar era, wage earners and farmers, have gained most.

The Emerging Mass Market

The substantial growth of income of wage earners and farmers during the postwar years also contributed to a more equal distribution of income. Significantly, in terms of the relative gain, the lower income classes have gained most during the past decades. According to a government survey, between 1963 and 1969 the average gain in income for all households was approximately ¥98,000 or almost 36 percent. Table 1.10 shows the increase in amount and percentage increase of the five income classes between 1963 and 1969.

A striking measure of the improvement of the standard of living in the postwar period is the very wide distribution of consumer durables. As Table 1.11 shows, in 1971 more than 82 percent of the households owned black-and-white television sets, more than 42 percent owned color sets, almost 94 percent owned washing machines and more than 91 percent owned refrigerators. Over a fourth of the families owned an automobile. Also noteworthy is the fact that there

TABLE 1.9

Average Annual Income of Agricultural Households
for Selected Years, 1955-70
(in thousands of yen)

	Nominal	Real
1955	358	453
1960	410	499
1965	761	761
1968	1,126	990
1969	1,250	1,076
1970	1,386	—

Source: Kokumin Seikatsu Tokei Nenpo, 1971, p. 70.

TABLE 1.10

Income Gains Reported by Five Income Classes
in Japan, 1963-69

Income Class	Increase in Income (in yen)	Percentage Increase
1	58,000	57.8
2	77,000	43.6
3	92,000	38.4
4	111,000	33.7
5	150,000	26.7

Source: Prime Minister's Office.

TABLE 1.11

Japanese Ownership of Selected
Consumer Durables, 1971
(in percentages)

	All Households	Agricultural Households	Nonagricultural Households	Urban Households*
Black-and-white TV	82.3	85.0	81.7	90.0
Color TV	42.3	31.1	45.2	30.4
Passenger cars	26.8	30.0	26.0	22.6
Refrigerators	91.2	87.7	92.2	92.5
Washing machines	93.6	93.4	93.7	92.1

*In cities with population of 50,000 or more, 1970.

Source: Kokumin Seikatsu Tokei Nenpo, 1971, p. 120.

is no significant difference in the rate of diffusion of consumer durables between urban and rural households.

Savings and Consumption Patterns

Having examined the salient features of the emerging mass consumer market in Japan let us now examine the consumption pattern. A well-know aspect of the Japanese economy has been a traditionally high rate of saving. During the past decade the average Japanese family saved roughly 20 percent of its discretionary income. Moreover, the savings rate has been increasing during the past three years. An average Japanese family has savings of over ¥1.6 million and this amount, too, has shown considerable growth during the past several years. Significantly, in contrast to the practice in the United States, over half of the savings are kept in the form of regular bank accounts; only 14 percent are in the form of securities of various types.

Now let us examine how the Japanese spend their income. Let us particularly note changes in the spending pattern of Japanese consumers. In this connection, we shall draw heavily on data provided by the annual household expenditure surveys conducted by the Japanese government. The Office of the Prime Minister conducts a Family Income and Expenditure Survey annually among a nationwide sample of nonagricultural families. The Ministry of Agriculture undertakes a similar study among agricultural households. These studies follow well-accepted research methodology and provide comprehensive and reliable data.

Tables 1.12 and 1.13 present summary data of household expenditures in absolute amounts for each of the major categories for over a decade for both urban, nonagricultural households, and rural agricultural households. Tables 1.14 and 1.15 present in index form the changes in each of the categories during the period under examination.

Several significant observations can be made about the data presented here: (1) the consumption level has increased steadily throughout the years indicated for urban and rural households, both absolutely and relatively; (2) the Engel's Coefficient, an important measure of the standard of living, steadily declined from 45 to 35.6 for urban households and from 49 to 32.4 for rural households during the years examined (since the lowest Engel's Coefficient in the prewar era was around 50, this is a rather significant achievement); (3) for both urban and rural households the most significant relative gains were made in the areas of housing and miscellaneous expenditure. The miscellaneous category includes expenditures for cultural,

TABLE 1.12

Household Expenditure Patterns of Nonagricultural Households
in Cities with Population of 50,000 or More, 1956-68

Year	Persons per Household	Total Living Expenditures	Food	Housing	Fuel and Light	Clothing	Miscellaneous	Engel's Coefficient	Living Expenditure Level* (1965=100)
			(monthly expenditures in yen)						
1956	4.61	23,958	10,786	1,625	1,225	2,920	7,402	45.0	64.4
1957	4.56	25,608	11,368	1,819	1,331	3,096	7,994	44.4	67.1
1958	4.57	27,171	11,898	2,239	1,353	3,135	8,546	43.8	71.5
1959	4.56	28,902	12,260	2,600	1,396	3,376	9,270	42.4	75.4
1960	4.51	31,276	13,000	2,790	1,597	3,755	10,134	41.6	78.9
1961	4.34	34,329	13,842	3,399	1,731	4,326	11,031	40.3	84.1
1962	4.29	38,587	15,063	3,951	1,906	4,933	12,734	39.0	88.9
1963	4.30	43,616	16,793	4,394	2,021	5,432	14,985	38.5	93.4
1964	4.28	47,834	18,139	4,703	2,171	5,683	17,138	37.9	98.7
1965	4.24	51,832	19,738	5,157	2,389	5,916	18,632	38.1	100.0
1966	4.17	56,097	20,836	5,686	2,554	6,206	20,815	37.1	103.9
1967	4.13	61,091	22,355	6,424	2,730	6,725	22,858	36.6	109.4
1968	4.06	66,440	23,665	7,665	2,867	7,338	24,906	35.6	121.5

*Indices of living expenditure are adjusted for the average number of persons per household and deflated by the consumer price index.

Source: The Annual Report on the Family Income and Expenditure Survey, 1968 (Tokyo: The Office of the Prime Minister, 1969), p. 32.

TABLE 1.13

Household Expenditure Patterns of Agricultural Households in Cities with Population of 50,000 or More, 1956-67

Year	Persons per Household	Total Living Expenditures	Food	Housing	Fuel and Light	Clothing	Miscellaneous	Engel's Coefficient	Living Expenditure Level* (1960=100)
			(monthly expenditures in yen)						
1956	6.23	25,475	12,483	1,917	1,250	2,883	6,942	49.0	86.8
1957	5.93	25,425	12,175	1,825	1,292	2,933	7,200	47.9	87.7
1958	5.86	25,817	12,225	1,950	1,233	2,925	7,483	47.4	89.9
1959	5.80	27,342	12,400	2,550	1,283	3,117	7,992	45.4	93.4
1960	5.70	29,542	12,717	3,100	1,433	3,467	8,825	43.0	100.0
1961	5.64	33,192	13,592	4,000	1,600	3,908	10,092	40.9	107.8
1962	5.52	36,733	14,492	4,392	1,842	4,325	11,682	39.5	114.7
1963	5.42	41,075	15,842	4,908	2,008	4,742	13,575	38.6	121.5
1964	5.31	46,258	17,608	5,717	2,200	5,117	15,616	38.1	130.8
1965	5.29	52,067	19,350	6,392	2,475	5,767	18,083	37.2	137.5
1966	5.18	57,471	20,828	7,117	2,655	6,055	20,816	36.2	143.8
1967	4.97	72,625	23,517	13,650	3,058	7,250	25,150	32.4	163.7

*Indices of living expenditure are adjusted for the average number of persons per household and deflated by the consumer price index.

Source: The Annual Report on the Family Income and Expenditure Survey, 1968 (Tokyo: The Office of the Prime Minister, 1969), p. 33.

TABLE 1.14

Indices of Expenditure Levels by Major Categories
for Urban Nonagricultural Households, 1956-68
(1965 = 100)

Year	Total Living Expenditures	Food	Housing	Fuel and Light	Clothing	Miscellaneous
1956	46.2	54.6	31.5	51.3	49.4	39.7
1957	49.4	57.6	35.3	55.7	52.3	42.9
1958	52.4	60.3	43.4	56.6	53.0	45.9
1959	55.8	62.1	50.4	58.4	57.1	49.8
1960	60.3	65.9	54.1	66.8	63.5	54.4
1961	66.2	70.1	65.9	72.5	73.1	59.2
1962	74.4	76.3	76.6	79.8	83.4	68.3
1963	84.1	85.1	85.2	84.6	91.7	80.4
1964	92.3	91.9	91.2	90.9	96.1	92.0
1965	100.0	100.0	100.0	100.0	100.0	100.0
1966	108.2	105.6	110.3	106.9	104.9	111.7
1967	117.9	113.3	124.6	114.3	113.7	122.7
1968	128.2	119.9	148.6	120.1	124.1	133.7

Source: The Annual Report on the Family Income and Expenditure Survey, 1968 (Tokyo: The Office of the Prime Minister, 1969), p. 32.

social-recreational, and educational activities. In both urban and rural households real expenditures for these categories about tripled during the period.

Finally, the data reveal very little difference in consumption levels between the urban nonagricultural and rural agricultural households. As already noted, the reader should also remember that despite the rapid rate of increase in consumption levels, the average propensity to save has been increasing. We mention parenthetically that nearly 93 percent of Japanese households have some form of savings: 85 percent have savings accounts, 74 percent have life insurance, and over 13 percent own stock.*

---

*A Survey of Consumption and Savings, 1968 (Tokyo: The Economic Planning Agency, 1968), pp. 153-159.

Let us now examine how the expenditure patterns vary according to income class. Table 1.16 presents the expenditure pattern by income quintile groups for the nationwide sample of nonagricultural households. As might be expected, the percent spent for food declines with the increase in the income level, and just the reverse trend is apparent for expenditure in the miscellaneous category. The highest income bracket allocated a little over 42 percent of the total expenditure in this latter category. In this group, the expenditure for cultural and recreational activities alone accounted for slightly over 8 percent of the total expenditure.

SOCIAL ASPECTS

Rapid economic progress has substantially improved the standard of living of the masses and has altered their mode of living rather

TABLE 1.15

Indices of Expenditure Levels by Major Categories
for Agricultural Households, 1956-67
(1965 = 100)

Year	Total Living Expenditures	Food	Housing	Fuel and Light	Clothing	Miscellaneous
1956	48.9	64.5	30.0	50.5	50.0	38.4
1957	48.8	62.9	28.6	52.2	50.9	39.8
1958	49.6	63.2	30.5	49.8	50.7	41.4
1959	52.5	64.1	39.9	51.8	51.0	44.2
1960	56.7	65.7	48.5	57.9	60.1	48.8
1961	63.7	70.2	62.6	64.6	67.8	55.8
1962	70.5	74.9	68.7	74.4	75.0	64.6
1963	78.9	81.9	76.8	81.1	82.2	75.1
1964	88.8	91.0	89.4	88.9	88.7	86.4
1965	100.0	100.0	100.0	100.0	100.0	100.0
1966	110.4	107.6	111.3	107.3	105.0	115.1
1967	139.5	121.5	213.5	123.6	125.7	139.1

Source: The Annual Report on the Family Income and Expenditure Survey, 1968 (Tokyo: The Office of the Prime Minister, 1969), p. 33.

TABLE 1.16

Yearly Average of Monthly Disbursements for Living Expenditures per Household by Monthly Income Quintile Groups, 1968
(in yen and percentages)

Annual Income Quintile Group	Total Living Expenditures	Food	Housing	Fuel and Light	Clothing	Miscellaneous
I. Less than 575,000	37,878(100)	15,797(41.7)	4,626(12.2)	2,170(5.7)	3,557(9.4)	11,722(31.0)
II. 575,000–764,000	50,108(100)	19,546(39.0)	6,236(12.5)	2,471(4.9)	5,039(10.1)	16,800(33.5)
III. 764,000–968,000	59,962(100)	22,179(37.0)	7,183(12.0)	2,647(4.4)	6,393(10.7)	21,589(36.0)
IV. 968,000–1,291,000	71,017(100)	24,422(34.4)	8,346(11.8)	2,902(4.1)	8,091(11.4)	27,177(38.3)
V. Over 1,291,000	93,550(100)	29,489(31.5)	9,427(10.1)	3,686(3.9)	11,501(12.3)	39,394(42.1)
Average	62,503(100)	22,286(35.7)	7,163(11.5)	2,795(4.5)	6,928(11.1)	23,330(37.3)

Source: The Annual Report on the Family Income and Expenditure Survey, 1968 (Tokyo: The Office of the Prime Minister, 1969), pp. 194-196.

drastically. The Japanese themselves are very aware of a new way of life and to describe fundamental changes made in Japanese life style, they use such terms as <u>shohi kakumei</u> or consumption revolution. Postwar changes include much more in the average Japanese view than mere material improvements. They mean a new way of life, with a greater amount of leisure time, emancipation from time-consuming daily household chores, and greater individual freedom. Indeed, the amenities of the middle class have finally come within the reach of the average family. Almost every aspect of life has been affected. For one thing, diet patterns have changed rather drastically. Per capita daily caloric intake has been steadily increasing—in 1968 it reached 2224. Qualitative changes are even more significant. The Japanese have departed from traditional diet patterns. In 1948, for example, 72 percent of the caloric intake of an average Japanese was derived from various types of cereal products, but this had declined to 42 percent by 1970. The consumption of rice has been steadily declining, while consumption of meat, eggs, and dairy products has been steadily increasing.

Even more significant are the rather drastic changes that are taking place in the attitudes of consumers. We shall now briefly examine salient social features of contemporary Japanese society.

Consumption Orientation

Traditionally, the Japanese culture emphasized aesthetic values and a nonmaterial orientation. Social position and prestige depended less on possessions of material wealth than on nonmaterial factors. While conspicuous consumption was not entirely unknown in Japan, it was not pervasive nor was it well-accepted. Frugality was emphasized as a great virtue and consumption was viewed contemptuously. Until recently, of course, frugality had not been a matter of choice for the masses. They simply could not afford much more than the bare necessities of life. This has radically changed. No longer is the desire for consumption held as evil, and something to be repressed. The cry for frugality is seldom heard. On the contrary, an average consumer is constantly exposed to mass media advertising.

Implicit in this change is the widespread recognition of the legitimacy of aspirations, of financial and material reward, and of a desire to make one's life more comfortable and pleasant. This is substantiated by a number of public opinion surveys. The traditional nonmaterial, almost puritanlike values, have now given way to those which emphasize materialism and consumption orientation. Closely related to the emergence of materialistic orientation is the search for private joy and immediate gratification of desires. This trend is particularly noticeable among the youth. Many Japanese youths have learned to tailor their ambitions to their realistic prospects and have begun to attach greater importance to family life and middle class amenities than to a career, professional success, or to ideas that their forefathers thought were of great significance.

Westernization

Throughout its history, Japan has borrowed heavily, though selectively, from foreign cultures. For centuries prior to the modern era, the Chinese influence had been dominant. For the last century, Western culture, particularly its technological component, has played a key role. Despite extensive cultural borrowing throughout the nation's history, Japan has retained much of its own tradition and has adapted what it borrowed from other cultures to fit its own traditions and needs. Indeed, the Japanese have shown an amazing degree of flexibility, and now feel nothing incongruent about selective acceptance of foreign cultures.

Since the end of World War II, the American influence has been particularly pervasive in almost every aspect of life. Let us examine a few examples to identify the extent to which Westernization has progressed in postwar Japan. For one thing, Western foods have become commonplace in the daily diet of an average Japanese. In fact, to many Japanese, particularly those living in urban areas, the diet patterns are more Western than traditionally Japanese. As can be seen from Table 1.17, the consumption of some Western-type food products experienced a significant increase between 1963 and 1969.

Equally significant is the trend toward Western-style living patterns. This trend is partially evidenced by the diffusion of Western-style furniture as presented in Table 1.18. As may be expected, there are some variations among different occupational groups. Farmers' households are least Westernized while Westernization has progressed most among individual proprietors and professionals. Also to be expected, there is a definite relationship between income level and ownership of the Western style of furniture. Furthermore, in almost all new homes built in recent years Western architectural features are incorporated. Of course the Westernization trend has not replaced, and is not likely to replace completely, Japan's traditional mode of living. On the contrary, with growing discretionary income, the Japanese have begun to develop dual patterns. Japanese consumers have selectively adopted Western styles of living, but at the same time have made a conscious effort to retain traditions for certain occasions. This stems from the Japanese view that although

TABLE 1.17

Annual Expenditure for Selected Food Products in
Japan for Selected Years, 1963-69
(in thousands of yen)

	1963	1965	1967	1969
Ham (100 g.)	31.49	31.44	34.88	40.23
Bacon (100 g.)	2.00	2.65	2.86	3.24
Milk (180 cc. bottles)	322.00	389.00	459.00	493.00
Butter (100 g.)	7.40	9.29	8.80	9.40
Cheese (100 g.)	3.50	5.10	8.68	10.50
Lettuce (100 g.)	—	12.93	20.65	29.30
Mayonnaise (100 g.)	13.40	17.50	20.80	26.30
Ketchup (100 g.)	7.48	9.35	11.18	11.80

Source: The Office of the Prime Minister.

the Western mode of living is highly functional and well suited for daily living, it lacks the beauty and charm associated with things that are traditionally Japanese. This is nowhere more evident than in the mode of dress. For work, the Japanese have totally adopted more functional Western-style clothing, but for ceremonial occasions, they still prefer the traditional kimono.

Education and Mass Media

An important characteristic of the Japanese consumer market is that it is one of the best informed in the world. The Japanese have traditionally placed a great deal of emphasis on education and during the past century Japan has developed an excellent formal system of education. The educational system was totally overhauled in the immediate aftermath of World War II and was modelled after the United States system. The literacy rate is nearly 100 percent. More significantly, 84 percent of those completing eight years of compulsory education go on to high school for another three years of education. One out of three high school graduates go on to college or its equivalent. Statistics provide convincing evidence that Japanese consumers are among the best educated in the world.

Another important feature of the Japanese market is the very wide diffusion of the mass media. Given the small size of the country

TABLE 1.18

Japanese Expenditure for Selected Western-Style
Furniture by Income Group, 1971
Nonagricultural and Agricultural
(in percentages)

Income of Nonagricultural Households (in yen)	Living Room Furniture	Dining Room Furniture	Beds
300,000 or less	2.4	1.8	6.6
300,000 - 599,999	8.9	8.0	11.5
600,000 - 899,999	10.4	16.5	16.6
900,000 - 1,199,999	19.8	28.2	26.4
1,200,000 - 1,499,999	30.0	37.7	31.1
1,500,000 - 1,799,999	37.9	43.5	37.1
1,800,000 or more	54.4	56.5	46.6
Average	23.8	29.4	26.4
Income of Agricultural Households (in yen)			
300,000 or less	—	—	—
300,000 - 599,999	7.4	7.0	7.4
600,000 - 899,999	7.0	12.8	9.8
900,000 - 1,199,999	20.9	21.4	18.4
1,200,000 - 1,499,999	21.3	21.7	19.9
1,500,000 - 1,799,999	32.0	32.0	17.1
1,800,000 or more	42.6	41.5	26.6
Average	16.3	18.2	19.6

Source: Economic Planning Agency.

and high population density, coupled with the characteristic curiosity of the Japanese, there is nowhere in the world where the mass media coverage is as extensive as in Japan. Given their importance to consumer marketing, let us examine the major characteristics of the media. First, let us look at the newspaper circulation. There are 117 newspapers with a combined circulation of 53 million (morning and evening editions combined). This is roughly one paper to every two people. Japan has several excellent newspapers with nationwide circulation. For example, Asahi boasts a daily circulation of 5.7 million copies, making it one of the largest newspapers in the world. Nearly 2,500 magazines are published each year, with a total of over 1.7 billion copies. Over half of these are weeklies. During the past year, nearly 18,000 different types of books were published.

In the area of broadcasting, we have already seen the wide diffusion of television sets among Japanese households. Homes in even the humblest hamlet in remote rural areas now have a television set, and several channels compete for the time and attention of the audience from early morning until late at night.

No doubt, a widespread and centrally controlled educational system and the mass media have contributed greatly to bridging the gap between classes as well as between various regions, and have helped instill egalitarian values. New ideas are accepted quickly and innovations catch on. Fashion news, in particular, spreads throughout the country with very little time lag. With the growth of mass media came the development of advertising which, in turn, stimulated the further growth of mass media.

To all the mass media, with the exception of NHK, the government-sponsored broadcasting agency, advertising provides the primary source of income. There are few countries in the world where there is such intensive advertising through mass media as in Japan. The postwar growth of advertising can be seen from Table 1.19. In 1970, the total advertising expenditure reached nearly ¥650 billion, which is roughly 1 percent of the nation's GNP. During the past ten years, the advertising expenditure almost quadrupled.

The total expenditure is divided between the media in the following way: newspapers account for approximately 35 percent; television, 33 percent; magazines, 5.6 percent; and radio is responsible for 4.4 percent. Altogether, the four major media account for approximately 78 percent of the total advertising expenditure, as reported by the Dentsu Advertising Agency in Tokyo in 1969. (See Table 1.20). Particularly remarkable is the very rapid growth of television as an advertising medium. Television now has become the single most important medium by which major consumer industries publicize their products; for example, the processed food industry spent nearly 68 percent of its total advertising budget on this single medium.

TABLE 1.19

Growth of Total Advertising Expenditure
in Japan, 1955-70
(in billions of yen)

Year	Total Amount
1955	60.9
1956	74.5
1957	94.0
1958	106.5
1959	145.6
1960	174.0
1961	211.0
1962	243.5
1963	298.2
1964	349.1
1966	383.1
1967	459.4
1968	532.0
1969	628.7
1970	650.0*

*Estimated.

Source: Dentsu Advertising Annual, 1970 (Tokyo: Dentsu Advertising Agency, 1971).

Likewise, the cosmetic industry spent 70 percent; the sundry goods industry, 60 percent; and the pharmaceutical industry, 54 percent.

Description of the growth of advertising expenditure alone tells only part of the story. Equally impressive is the marked improvement in the quality of advertising. The Japanese have applied their recognized artistic ability to creating most attractive advertisements.

Convenience Orientation

An important trend in the Japanese consumer market is an increasing preference for convenience. This is apparent in almost every aspect of daily life. The widespread diffusion of consumer durables has drastically changed the role of the housewife in a typical

TABLE 1.20

Distribution of Advertising Expenditure
by Major Media, 1970

Medium	Amount (¥ billion)	Percentage
Newspaper	188.4	35.4
Television	174.5	32.9
Magazines	29.7	5.6
Radio	23.3	4.4
Others	115.3	21.7
Total	532.1	100.0

Source: Dentsu Advertising Agency, 1971.

Japanese household. No longer do housewives have to spend many hours in performing the drudgery of household chores. The desire for convenience is also very apparent in the growing expenditure for processed packaged foods. Household expenditure for processed foods has been growing at an average rate of roughly 8 percent during the last several years. Dehydrated packaged noodles, instant coffee, packaged curry sauce, and frozen foods are among the products that have shown a very high rate of growth. It has been projected that frozen foods will achieve an extraordinarily high growth rate during the 1970s.

A number of factors contribute to the growing preference for convenience: (1) the basic change in the value system, particularly the change in the traditional role of women as obedient housewives who gladly perform the household chores; (2) the trend toward Westernization and erosion of the traditional family structure; and (3) the growing number of housewives now gainfully employed, primarily on a part-time basis.

Leisure Orientation

A significant development among Japanese consumers is the growing enjoyment of leisure. This is not surprising in view of two developments: reduction in working hours and the growing amount of discretionary income. For the past several years working hours have been steadily declining. The five-day work week is gradually being adopted by a substantial number of large enterprises. On the home front, with the advent of consumer durables housewives have been relieved of time-consuming daily household chores. Expenditure for leisure activities almost doubled between 1966 and 1971. Now, as can be seen in Table 1.21, the total leisure market is estimated to be over $10 billion. Leisure-related expenditures reached nearly 23 percent of the total household budget in the early 1970s and expenditure for leisure-related activities has been rising at the rate of 20 percent a year during 1966-71.

Meantime, the pattern of leisure activities has undergone significant changes. For one thing, the emphasis is now gradually shifting from passive pastimes to more active recreational and cultural activities. Until recently, the favorite pastime was simply relaxing at home, reading or watching television; but now a greater number of people are becoming more actively engaged in hobbies. Similarly, in sports the interest is gradually shifting from spectator sports to golf, bowling, and other sports requiring active participation. It is estimated that a million people play golf regularly. Another sport that has gained rapid acceptance is bowling. In 1965, there were only 221 bowling alleys in Japan. The number has grown sevenfold, and in 1973 it was estimated that there were 5 million people who bowled regularly. The bowling population is projected to reach 10 million by 1975.

TABLE 1.21

Leisure-Related Expenditure by Urban Households
for Selected Years, 1965-70
(in yen)

	1965	1968	1970	Percent Increase 1965-70
Leisure expenditure	119,400	170,157	225,555	88.9
Total consumer expenditure	621,090	797,293	993,502	59.7
Leisure expenditure as percentage of total expenditure	19.2	21.3	22.7	*

*Not relevant.

Source: Ministry of Welfare.

Another significant leisure or recreational activity is sightseeing. During 1970 a total of 83 million people made one-day sightseeing trips. On the average, the Japanese family made 3.5 one-day, out-of-town pleasure trips. Also, during the same year, the national parks attracted a total of 270 million people, roughly 2.7 times the nation's total population. It is interesting to note that one-third of these made overnight trips with their families, while some 36 percent participated in group tours. With the advent of an affluent mass market, there emerged a tremendously attractive leisure market in Japan.

PROBLEMS FACING JAPANESE CONSUMERS

The phenomenal economic growth during the past decade and a half has not been a total blessing. Japanese consumers have had to pay a price for the tremendous improvement in their standard of living. Moreover, the standard of living has not achieved balanced improvement. In some areas, notably in education, mass media dispersal, and quality of consumer durables, Japan is among the most advanced nations, while in others she lags behind.

Let us now consider major problems confronting the Japanese consumers. First is the constant rise in price levels. This has been particularly notable at the consumer level. Between 1965 and 1970, the overall consumer price index went up nearly 31 percent. During the same period, the wholesale price index increased by 11.3 percent. Food prices increased by 34 percent and rents by 45 percent. The constant increase of the price level has posed a serious and agonizing problem for the average Japanese consumer. Government efforts to arrest the rise in consumer price level have not been successful and the outlook is by no means bright. Many Japanese consumers are concerned that the steadily inflationary trend is gradually eroding the standard of living.

Even more serious is the rapid rate with which the quality of life is degenerating because of environmental deterioration. The problem is obviously most acute in large urban centers with high population density. The Japanese coined a new word, kogai (public nuisance) to describe it. Almost every environmental degradation is present in Japan, including traffic congestion, air and water pollution, high noise levels, and so on, which result from Japan's rapid postwar growth. Population density, particularly in the highly industrialized areas of Japan, has created very serious problems of waste disposal.

Air pollution in major industrial centers is among the worst problems. Industrial water pollution has been designated as the cause for serious illness, and has activated a citizens' movement against the corporations that are allegedly responsible for such pollution. In fact, citizens have become so concerned that it is becoming increasingly difficult for many manufacturers to find suitable plant locations. While some legal measures have been taken to control environmental pollution, they have had minimum impact so far and the environment continues to deteriorate. There seems to be little hope for an immediate solution.

Another fundamental problem is the inadequate social infrastructure. Even a cursory observation reveals that such public facilities as roads, sewage disposal, and parks are glaringly inadequate throughout Japan. Road conditions alone are the worst among major advanced nations. Despite the presence of some superhighways, only about a fourth of what are known as national highways are paved. In all areas less than 11 percent of the roads are paved. The Japanese government, concerned with these conditions, has begun to stress public expenditure to improve the infrastructure. There are signs of gradual improvement, but Japan has a long way to go to reach even the Western European level.

Another major problem facing the Japanese citizen is the inadequate social security and welfare system, particularly for the aged. This system, as broadly conceived, is extremely inadequate in Japan, both in quantitative and qualitative terms. The expenditure for social welfare is the lowest among all advanced nations. The care of the aged, alone, is becoming a critical social problem because of the breakdown of the traditional family system.

The very rapid economic growth, urbanization, and the accompanying problems have brought about emotional and psychological problems as well. Typical problems that are associated with highly urbanized and industrialized societies have begun to emerge. The Japanese society has become fast-paced and tension-ridden. A growing number of people have come to feel alienated, isolated, and frustrated. This sense of alienation is particularly high in the major urban centers, especially among the youth who have migrated into the cities from rural areas. This has resulted in an increase in antisocial behavior. Although the crime rate is still among the lowest in advanced nations, it is rising.

Recent public opinion surveys summarize rather eloquently concern about these trends. A nationwide opinion survey conducted by the Office of the Prime Minister in 1970 asked the respondents to give an overall evaluation of what the postwar economic growth has meant to the average citizen. Interestingly, only 29 percent said that benefits outweighed negative aspects, 14 percent said the opposite, and the rest were ambivalent.

Concern for the quality of life cannot be adequately treated without consideration of the housing problem. While Japanese consumers have experienced dramatic improvements in a number of respects, there is one area where advances fall far short of the need; this is in the area of housing. High concentration of population in major urban centers, skyrocketing land prices, and the rapid increase in the number of nuclear families have contributed to serious housing shortages. Land prices in the six major cities have averaged a sixfold increase in the 1960s. Naturally, some of the most attractive areas have experienced price appreciation many times that. Home ownership, in fact, has become a lifetime goal for the masses.

In Tokyo, where the housing plight is the worst, 40 percent of the residents own their homes, 48 percent rent from private parties, 7 percent live in houses provided by companies, and 5 percent live in public housing. Over 62 percent of the privately owned homes have space of 550 square feet or less; over 90 percent of the rented houses are smaller than 550 square feet. No wonder, then, that housing has become a source of major concern. A recent survey reveals that 37 percent of the heads of households that occupied their own homes were dissatisfied with their present housing conditions. Understandably, nearly 60 percent of those who live in rented quarters reported that they were seriously dissatisfied with their present housing conditions. High concentration of population in urban centers has, of course, encouraged home building in suburban areas. Almost all private and public housing developments are now taking place in the suburbs that are at a considerable distance from the centers, creating rather serious commuting problems. For those living in major metropolitan areas, particularly in Tokyo and Osaka, it is not uncommon to spend an hour commuting each way. The government has been making some effort to alleviate the serious housing shortage in urban areas, but the problem is far from solved and still remains a national issue of utmost concern.

THE RISING TIDE OF CONSUMERISM

A significant trend that no marketing executive can ignore in contemporary Japan is the rising tide of consumerism. The consumer movement, organized and led primarily by housewives, appeared in the immediate aftermath of World War II. Its activists have been making continuing efforts, though not always successfully, to protect what they consider consumer interests. During the last two or three years, however, the consumer movement in Japan has gained considerable strength.

Several forces are responsible for the surge of consumerism in Japan. The first and foremost is the emergence of a mass consumer market and those forces of change that have been described earlier. For the first time, Japanese consumers have gained a power of considerable magnitude in the marketplace. With the advent of a mass consumption society, however, came aggressive sales promotion efforts by major manufacturers as well as marketing intermediaries. A wide array of new products appeared in the marketplace and consumers were deluged by mass media advertising. Exaggerated, if not false, claims were made and overly aggressive sales efforts have become commonplace. Uninformed consumers have often become the prey of these undesirable marketing tactics.

Another force is the rising consumer price discussed earlier. With conflict between rising expectations to improve the standard of living on one hand, and inflationary pressures on the other, consumers have become more and more discriminating. The third factor is concern for product safety. Such concern has manifested itself toward a variety of products, ranging from pharmaceuticals to foods to automobiles. Here the influence of the mass media cannot be denied. In a number of these incidents, the mass media have cooperated, their coverage giving the movement further impetus. Of course, the concern for product safety is by no means unrelated to the citizen's concern for general environmental deterioration.

Still another force is the rising consumerism in the United States. No doubt the consumer movement promoted by Ralph Nader has stimulated the movement in Japan. Of all these factors leading to rising consumerism, none is more basic than the growing awareness by consumers of their power in the marketplace, if properly organized.

With this background Japanese consumers, particularly housewives, began to exert themselves. Organized efforts by consumers were directed against a major United States soft drink bottler for its alleged use of cyclamates (the accusation turned out to be false); automobile manufacturers for defective automobiles; a major cosmetic manufacturer for resale price maintenance and high prices; and manufacturers of color televisions for high domestic prices in comparison with export prices. Perhaps none was more effective than the protest against major manufacturers of color television sets. Disturbed by the presence of substantial differences in the price of presumably similar sets for export and those for the domestic market, consumers waged the most effective campaign ever undertaken in Japan. It was successful in persuading a major manufacturer to change the price structure. Other major manufacturers followed suit.

While consumerism in Japan has its own problems and limitations, it has demonstrated its power and the marketing executives can ignore it only at their own peril. The Japanese government is moving, though slowly, to enact a number of legislative measures to protect the consumer.

CHAPTER

2

THE JAPANESE DISTRIBUTION SYSTEM: AN OVERVIEW

One of the most perplexing features to American businessmen interested in penetrating the Japanese consumer market is Japan's complex system of distribution. This system has evolved over the centuries and until recently has not been affected to any measurable degree by the modernization process. In the last decade or so, however, with the advent of the mass market, a number of major innovations are now being introduced into the once tradition-bound Japanese distribution sector. These very dynamic and innovative developments present opportunities as well as threats for American businessmen interested in Japan. Considerable opportunity is offered by these changes because American experience, if applied carefully, could give an important competitive edge to American firms.

Whereas these innovative elements are proceeding at a very rapid rate, there is danger in exaggerating such developments. Traditional patterns, despite the aggressive onslaught of new forces, have demonstrated considerable survival power. The customary elements are still too important to ignore. A number of American companies have experienced disastrous results by ignoring the old ways, which are still deeply entrenched. Misguided by the apparent acceptance of innovative forces into thinking that traditional elements were considerably weakened, some American managers decided, almost blindly, to cast their lot with those innovative forces—with calamitous results. A real challenge for an American firm is in designing an appropriate marketing strategy for a specific product, carefully weighing the strengths and weaknesses of both traditional and modern elements in the Japanese marketing system. In this and the ensuing two chapters, we shall examine salient characteristics of the Japanese distribution system, including changes that are now being introduced.

GROWTH OF THE DISTRIBUTION SYSTEM

Throughout the postwar decades, the distribution sector has kept up with Japan's rapid economic growth. This sector's contribution to the net national product increased from ¥919 billion in 1951 to over ¥8,000 billion* in 1971, recording a ninefold growth and slightly exceeding the growth rate of the net national product during the same period.

As can be seen from Table 2.1, both the wholesale and retail sectors have grown in the past two decades. The number of wholesale establishments more than doubled; the average sales per store more than quadrupled. Even in the retail sector, the number of stores increased 30 percent and the sales per store more than tripled.

The number of people gainfully employed in the distribution sector also has increased substantially. By 1971, over 8.9 million people were employed by marketing intermediaries. Since this figure does not include persons engaged in marketing activities in manufacturing and other service firms, the total number of people who are actually performing marketing functions in Japan is considerably greater.

DISTINCTIVE FEATURES OF THE MARKETING SYSTEM

There are several distinct features to the Japanese marketing system. One characteristic is that it is highly fragmented, with a large number of small establishments.

Fragmentation

According to the latest Commercial Census there are more than 277,000 wholesale establishments in Japan. A typical wholesaler averages about $600,000 in annual sales and has eleven employees. Even the wholesale sector is dominated by small establishments, as can be seen from Table 2.2. Nearly 45 percent of the wholesalers in Japan have four employees or less. Almost three-quarters of the total had nine employees or less. In fact, there are only 8,000

---

*Denominations are given in the Japanese system, in which 1,000 million equals the American billion and 1,000 billion equals the American trillion.

TABLE 2.1

Growth of Wholesale and Retail Sectors, 1952-68

Year	Number of Establishments (in thousands)	Adjusted* Sales per Store (¥ million)	Average Employees per Store	Sales per Employee (¥10,000)
		Wholesale Sector		
1952	131.2	50.53	6.27	807
1954	155.3	56.78	6.70	848
1956	171.4	69.23	7.33	944
1958	185.7	78.51	8.15	963
1960	215.9	87.05	8.70	1,001
1962	218.1	129.46	9.69	1,336
1964	223.8	174.86	11.20	1,562
1966	279.7	181.84	10.80	1,666
1968	276.6	226.03	10.93	2,069
		Retail Sector		
1952	1,079.7	2.56	2.13	120
1954	1,189.1	3.03	2.26	134
1956	1,201.3	3.58	2.56	143
1958	1,244.6	4.02	2.63	153
1960	1,288.3	4.51	2.71	167
1962	1,272.0	5.96	2.79	206
1964	1,304.5	6.82	2.92	233
1966	1,375.4	7.41	3.05	243
1968	1,389.2	8.51	3.05	279

*The wholesale and retail sales reported here have been adjusted by the wholesale price index and consumer price index, respectively, to remove the effects of inflation.

Source: Wagakuni no Shōgyō, 1969 [Commerce in Japan, 1969] (Tokyo: The Ministry of International Trade and Industry, 1970), p. 12.

TABLE 2.2

Wholesale and Retail Establishments in Japan
by Size, 1970
(in percentages)

Number of Employees	Wholesale Establishments	Retail Establishments
1- 2	21.3	64.0
3- 4	23.3	22.5
5- 9	29.2	9.6
10-19	15.3	2.6
20-29	4.6	0.6
30-49	3.3	0.4
50-99	2.0	0.2
100 & over	1.0	0.1
Total	100.0	100.0

Source: Commercial Census, 1971.

wholesale establishments, or roughly 3 percent of the total, having fifty employees or more.

Naturally, fragmentation is even worse in the retailing sector. There were 1,389,000 retail establishments in 1968, and they averaged no more than $30,000 in annual sales, with three employees. Since the Japanese population is slightly over 100 million, there is one retail store for about every seventy persons. As is evident in Table 2.2, stores with four employees or less accounted for nearly 87 percent of the 1.39 million establishments. A further indication of the predominance of small-scale stores is that nearly half of all retail stores were no larger than 200 square feet, and nearly three-quarters consisted of establishments with floor space of roughly 300 square feet or less.

Another evidence which gives some insight into the operations of a typical small-scale retail establishment is the number of customers who make a purchase in any given day. Table 2.3 provides us with the number of customers who made a purchase in one day during a typical seven-day period.

The existence of a large number of small retail stores is nowhere better illustrated than in food retailing. At present, there are more than 710,000 stores handling food products (in contrast to 320,000 in the United States). These account for more than half of

TABLE 2.3

Number of Customers per Day, 1970

Type of Store	Number of Customers
Food	228
Meat	166
Vegetables	165
Cosmetics	145
Stationery	90
Furniture	75
Ladies' and children's wear	73
Retail average	104

Source: Commercial Census, 1971, p. 32.

the total number of retail establishments in Japan and approximately 40 percent of the retail sales. The average annual sales of these shops is less than $25,000. On a daily basis, this is around $70.

The Pivotal Position of Wholesalers

Another notable feature of the Japanese distribution system is that traditionally the wholesalers occupied a pivotal position. They enjoyed dominance over manufacturers as well as retailers. Wholesalers' preeminence in the traditional distribution structure stems from the following considerations which have long prevailed in Japan. First, the manufacturing sector, particularly in the consumer product categories, had consisted of a myriad of small-scale establishments with limited outlets and virtually no managerial or marketing capabilities of their own. Wholesalers traditionally filled this void, and often advanced capital to help such manufacturers purchase raw materials and augment their working capital. Above all, they almost exclusively provided distribution functions. Small manufacturers thus were heavily dependent on large wholesalers.

Second, the presence of a large number of small retailers has been an important factor. Lacking financial resources, they, too, were limited in their ability to procure merchandise directly from small manufacturers. Wholesalers have traditionally extended liberal credit to small retailers, without which many of them would not have survived.

Third, wholesalers have been willing and capable of assuming other risks in their dealings with their suppliers as well as with their customers. These have included carrying inventory and providing transportation and storage. For these reasons, wholesalers have occupied the dominant position in the Japanese distribution system. This has been true in almost every type of consumer goods, ranging from foods, apparel, cosmetics, and drugs to all manner of sundries. In this way wholesalers have performed important functions, effectively linking a myriad of small manufacturers with a large number of small retailers. Both looked to wholesalers for knowledge of the market, contacts in the market, and financial assistance.

The Many Levels of Distributors

The Japanese distribution system is highly complex and circuitous. Merchandise, particularly consumer goods, must pass through multiple levels of marketing intermediaries, each performing narrow and highly specialized functions. This is particularly the case with the wholesaling sector. It is not uncommon for merchandise to pass through several different levels or types of wholesaling—primary, secondary, regional and local. The statistics are revealing in this regard. The 277,000 wholesalers are broken down into three categories. (1) Ten percent buy from producers and sell directly to industrial, institutional, or foreign users. Nearly 32,000 establishments, or 17.9 percent, buy from suppliers and sell directly to retailers. These are the largest categories of primary wholesalers. (2) The so-called intermediary wholesalers, comprising 11 percent of the total, buy from and sell to other wholesalers. (3) As many as 65,000, accounting for 37.1 percent, are secondary wholesalers who buy from other wholesalers and sell to various users. These and the remaining details are presented in Table 2.4.

Naturally, the complexity of the channels varies widely among various product categories. For illustrative purposes, Table 2.5 provides a few examples. When analyzed by number of establishments, it will be noted that most of the dealings are by wholesalers who buy from wholesalers and sell to retailers or those who buy from producers and sell directly to retailers (all but textiles). When the analysis is by percent of total volume, there is no common pattern for the various product groups.

The Limited Number of Customers

A wholesaler tends to have a limited number of customers that he deals with on a regular basis. An average wholesaler who buys

TABLE 2.4

Types of Wholesaling Activities, 1970

	Percent of Establishments	Percent of Total Sales Volume
Primary wholesalers		
Buy from producers and sell to industrial and institutional users	10.0	16.9
Buy from producers and sell to retailers	17.9	13.0
Buy from producers and sell to wholesalers	11.3	23.0
Intermediary wholesalers		
Buy from wholesalers and sell to wholesalers	11.0	9.2
Secondary wholesalers		
Buy from wholesalers and sell to industrial users	13.8	5.8
Buy from wholesalers and sell to foreign users	0.3	0.3
Buy from wholesalers and sell to retailers	23.0	10.0
Others	12.8	21.7
	100.0	100.0

Source: Commercial Census, 1971.

from other wholesalers will sell to perhaps 22 wholesalers and these sell directly to retailers (on the average to 61 retail outlets). Obviously, the smaller the unit, the fewer the customers. Table 2.6 presents a detailed picture.

Wholesalers' Dependence on Credit

Wholesalers, too, make heavy use of credit extended by suppliers of merchandise, regardless of their sources of merchandise. On the

TABLE 2.5

Wholesale Establishments According to Customer Groups, 1970

	Textiles		Agricultural Products		Foods		Cosmetics, Pharmaceuticals		Furniture	
	Percent of Establish-ments	Percent of Total Volume	Percent of Establish-ments	Percent of Total Volume	Percent of Establish-ments	Percent of Total Volume	Percent of Establish-ments	Percent of Total Volume	Percent of Establish-ments	Percent of Total Volume
Buy from producers and sell to re-tailers and whole-salers	7.1	14.1	2.9	3.3	1.9	1.5	7.0	8.4	9.0	11.3
Buy from producers and sell directly to retailers	9.6	5.8	25.2	32.5	26.5	11.5	23.9	25.4	26.0	28.7
Buy from producers and sell to other wholesalers	24.7	33.6	13.4	15.0	8.9	25.4	8.5	11.7	17.6	19.2
Buy from wholesalers and sell to other wholesalers	19.1	16.2	9.4	9.1	8.5	19.7	7.2	3.9	8.0	6.9
Buy from wholesalers and sell to retailers	30.3	13.0	27.7	22.0	39.5	28.1	30.6	12.4	28.1	18.1
Others	9.2	17.4	11.4	18.1	14.6	13.8	22.8	38.2	11.3	15.8

Source: Commercial Census, 1971.

TABLE 2.6

Average Number of Customers by Wholesaler Size, 1970

Number of Employees	Selling to Wholesalers	Selling to Retailers
1-4	8	26
5-9	17	63
10-19	31	78
20-49	54	135
50-99	93	179
100 & over	174	288

Source: Commercial Census, 1971.

average, less than 17 percent of the wholesalers' purchases are paid for in cash. Over half are paid for with promissory notes. Typically, the period of such a note is 60 to 90 days, but sometimes it is extended to as long as 120 days. The remainder are sold on regular credit, which generally comes due at the end of each month. Similarly, as can be seen from the bottom section of Table 2.7, about 20 percent of the volume handled by a typical wholesaler is sold for cash.

CHANGES IN THE WHOLESALING SYSTEM

During the past decade or so, Japanese wholesalers have been under tremendous pressures. Their once preeminent position has been seriously challenged and a number of significant changes have taken place. A number of key consumer industries have seen the emergence of large-scale manufacturing firms with rather sophisticated marketing capabilities, and many of these firms have now established vertically integrated and controlled distribution channels. In some cases they have assumed many of the wholesaling functions themselves, either by bypassing the existing wholesalers or by bringing the once-independent wholesalers under their own control. Certainly, these large manufacturing firms are much less dependent on wholesalers than small manufacturers have been previously. In many cases large manufacturers now insist that their wholesalers be exclusive dealers and often dictate the terms under which merchandise is to be resold. In some cases large manufacturers now own equity interest

TABLE 2.7

Wholesalers' Methods of Payment for Purchases
and Receipts for Sales by Size of Firm, 1970

Wholesalers' Purchases

Size of Firm* (Number of Employees)	Cash	Promissory Note	Regular Credit	Total
All	16.7	52.2	31.2	100
1- 4	27.9	38.6	33.5	100
5- 9	20.3	45.2	34.5	100
10-19	17.2	49.6	33.2	100
20-49	16.4	50.7	32.9	100
50-99	15.7	49.8	34.4	100
100 & more	14.9	57.5	27.6	100

Wholesalers' Receipts for Sales

	Cash	Promissory Note	Regular Credit	Total
All	19.1	50.2	30.7	100
1- 4	30.6	34.7	34.7	100
5- 9	22.9	40.3	36.8	100
10-19	20.1	43.0	36.9	100
20-49	18.4	47.6	34.0	100
50-99	18.8	50.6	30.6	100
100 & more	17.1	57.9	25.1	100

*Based on percent of volume.

Source: Commercial Census, 1971, p. 33.

in some of their wholesalers; and among these wholesalers it is not uncommon for representatives of the manufacturer to occupy top management positions.

At the same time, the emergence of large-scale retailing chains has also contributed to the reduction of the wholesalers' power. These large-scale chains have begun to assert their growing power vis-à-vis their wholesalers, and at the same time they have begun to assume some of the key wholesaling functions themselves.

There is a growing trend among large retail chains, if they do not buy directly from large manufacturers, to concentrate their purchases with a few large wholesalers. These developments, coupled with improved communication and transportation methods, have deprived wholesalers of many of their traditional functions. At least some of the traditional wholesaling functions now are being performed with greater effectiveness and efficiency by large manufacturers or by retailers (or both). Of course, this situation is by no means found in every industry, but it is becoming increasingly common, particularly in mass-produced consumer products.

We should note at the outset that wholesalers, unlike large manufacturers, had been left to their own devices in recovering from wartime destruction and dislocation. It is readily understandable that this was a difficult task for many of them. However, the wholesaling sector has by and large been oblivious to the rather basic changes that have been taking place in its environment during the last decade and a half. Particularly serious has been its inability to respond quickly and effectively to the new demands and functions created by these changes.

The Failure of Many Wholesalers to Adapt

A good case in point is the failure of the majority of the wholesalers to perform adequately the task of market development for the new products that have been introduced continually by large manufacturers in the postwar years. Many wholesalers apparently felt the performance of such a task was beyond what they perceived as proper wholesaling functions. Wholesalers' reluctance or even refusal to develop markets for new products invited manufacturers' encroachment into this sector and often led to eventual control of distribution channels by the manufacturers.

Like small retailers, the average wholesaler has been very complacent. This point is clearly demonstrated in the retailers' evaluation of their wholesalers in a study of small retail establishments commissioned by the Ministry of International Trade and Industry. While the retailers included in the study felt that their wholesalers were performing traditional wholesaling functions, such as delivery services, rather well, in other areas the retailers' evaluation of wholesalers' services was less than enthusiastic. For example, one-third of the 1,426 retailers interviewed felt that wholesalers gave mediocre or inadequate advice on merchandising, and nearly 23 percent reported that they gave no guidance at all in this area.

In the area of dissemination of useful market or industry information, 37 percent of the retailers interviewed felt that the wholesalers' services were inadequate, and nearly 25 percent reported that they did not receive any information whatsoever. Similarly, in the area of advertising and promotion only 17 percent were satisfied with the amount and the quality of guidance and assistance given by their wholesalers, and over 50 percent reported that they did not receive any help in this regard. In the area of financial assistance only slightly over 14 percent felt that they received either excellent or satisfactory service. Details of retailers' evaluations of the various services provided by their wholesalers are presented in Table 2.8.

It is evident from these data that wholesalers have tended in the past to depend complacently on personal relationships with their retailers, as the latter have done with their customers, and they have largely failed to improve their services and their efficiencies.

TABLE 2.8

Small Retailers' Evaluation of Services Provided by Wholesalers in Selected Areas, 1968

	Percent of 1,426 Respondents Replying					
	Excellent	Satisfactory	Mediocre	Inadequate	Not Provided at All	Don't Know
Delivery service	52.4	30.8	6.9	2.0	6.3	1.6
Merchandising advice	12.0	28.2	23.6	10.2	22.8	4.1
Advice on pricing	11.0	21.8	28.3	9.0	25.3	4.6
Market and industry information	11.1	23.1	23.7	13.5	24.7	3.9
Financial assistance	3.3	11.8	7.1	11.0	61.5	5.3
Return privileges	20.1	30.4	16.0	11.2	19.0	3.3
Advertising and and promotional assistance	4.3	12.9	16.6	11.2	50.5	4.5

Source: Adapted from Shogyō Ryutsu Kozo Chōsa [A study of the distribution structure] (Tokyo: Ryutsu Mondai Kenkyu Kyokai, 1968), pp. 84-88.

Seldom has the average wholesaler questioned his continued viability in the rapidly changing environment. But not all wholesalers have been idle in the face of their eroding power. To meet these rapidly changing conditions, some progressive wholesalers are taking a number of concrete steps, which we shall now examine.

Adaptive Behavior of Progressive Wholesalers

In response to rather dramatic changes in the environment, progressive wholesalers are making efforts to maintain their viability. Some are reorienting their functions, organization, and methods of operation to serve the needs of large-scale mass merchandising firms. These mass merchandising firms are capable of buying directly from large manufacturers; however, with the rapid expansion, their financial position is not always sound. These factors tend to provide new opportunities for wholesalers. Of course, to serve these emerging mass merchandising firms, it is essential for wholesalers to undergo rather fundamental changes in their modus operandi. Several new ways of operating have been developed: (1) A number of wholesalers have created special departments to serve the specific needs of large mass merchandising firms. A few more are making unusual efforts to develop merchandise lines that are particularly suitable to those needs.

(2) Large primary wholesalers have organized smaller secondary wholesalers on a selective basis into a loosely coordinated network of affiliates. The large wholesalers are making these efforts in the belief that, given the overwhelming number of small retail establishments, small secondary wholesalers will continue to exist in the future. The primary wholesalers, as the nucleus, extend various types of assistance, including financial and managerial participation, to the secondary wholesalers that are affiliated with the group.

(3) The third approach is an extension of the second—the formation of voluntary chains. According to the most recent statistics, there are 64 wholesaler-sponsored voluntary chains with slightly over 17,000 retail outlets in their membership, an average chain having some 300 retail stores. The following are examples of the concrete measures being taken by some progressive wholesalers.

No longer do progressive wholesalers confine their efforts to a narrow range of traditional activities. They are seeking to analyze what broad merchandising and marketing functions they can perform for different customer groups in a rapidly changing environment.

Moreover, increasingly progressive wholesalers are making special efforts to develop their own lines of merchandise. They have become much more sensitive to the consumer's needs and desires, and some have begun to assume the role of interpreters of consumer taste to the manufacturers. A few very large wholesalers have also developed private brands to improve their competitive advantages.

Traditionally, wholesalers have relied almost exclusively on apprentice personnel. Apprentices are recruited from persons with a minimum of education and often stay with the same establishment for life. While imbued with a strong sense of loyalty, they often lack a broad perspective and their growth potentials are often quite limited. To overcome these problems, a number of large, progressive wholesalers have begun to recruit college graduates and to streamline their personnel and management systems to allow greater flexibility.

Finally, a number of firms have undertaken improvements in their ability to perform logistics and storage functions. A number of progressive wholesalers have cooperated in establishing modern physical distribution centers in an easily accessible location. In the past, storage facilities had been concentrated in busy commercial areas with growing traffic congestion and their efficiency had begun to suffer. To avoid costly traffic problems, with their delays and inconveniences, some wholesalers have moved part of their operations to the suburbs, where they have created modern storage and warehouse facilities. At the time of this writing, a dozen or so modern wholesale centers were in operation and were enjoying considerable success.

A gulf is widening between wholesalers who are quickly losing competitive ability and those who are progressive and becoming revitalized. It appears that the latter tend to be large firms; it is the smaller and marginal ones that are losing ground.

Even in 1970, nearly one-fourth of the wholesalers had no employees, but in 1972 these wholesalers accounted for but 10 percent of total wholesale sales. The future of wholesaling in Japan indeed looks confused. Large, progressive and well-managed dealers are likely to dominate the scene; and smaller, inefficient and poorly managed wholesalers, who have enjoyed patronage based largely on their personal relationships with small retailers, are expected to decline sharply.

THE RETAILING SECTOR

Retail establishments still account for 83 percent of all stores in Japan. Of the 1.4 million retail establishments, about 70 percent are ordinary independent retail outlets. Table 2.9 summarizes the relative importance of each of the major types of retail establishments based on its sales as a percent of total retail sales in 1970.

TABLE 2.9

Relative Importance of
Retail Outlets in Japan, 1970

	Total Retail Sales (¥ billion)	Percentage of Total
Department stores	1,865	11.9
Supermarkets	2,000	12.7
Ordinary retail stores	10,770	69.8
Installment department stores	344	2.2
Others	526	3.4
Total	15,704	100.0

Source: Japan Textile Research Institute, 1971

Fragmentation

We have already noted that the Japanese retail sector is highly fragmented. Less than one-quarter of all retail establishments have regular paid employees, but it is important to note that these stores account for 73 percent of total sales. The larger stores are, however, becoming increasingly important. (See Table 2.10)

The percentage distribution presented in Table 2.11 further verifies this trend. The number of retail stores having only one or two employees has decreased considerably between 1964 and 1970, whereas the number of all categories of stores with more than three employees has increased. When we use another measure of size—floor space for sales—the trend is similar. During the five-year period between 1962 and 1967, the very small stores with sales space of 19 square meters or less declined whereas those with 30 or more square meters increased. (See Table 2.12.)

The following four tables present salient characteristics of various types of stores. In looking at Table 2.13, we note that in all but department stores, there is a very large concentration of small stores. Table 2.14 presents the relative importance of various types of stores. As noted earlier, independent retail outlets account for the preponderance of total sales. In Table 2.15 we note a substantial difference in operating efficiency among various types of stores. In terms of sales per employee, the department stores rank highest at ¥8.6 million, followed by self-service stores. Significantly, the sales

TABLE 2.10

Number of Retail Stores With and Without Paid
Employees, 1958 and 1968
(in percentages)

	Establishments 1958	Establishments 1968	Total Sales 1958	Total Sales 1968
Retail outlets without employees	80.4	76.6	34.4	27.1
Retail outlets with employees	19.6	23.4	65.6	72.9

Source: Commercial Census, 1971.

per employee in department stores is almost three times that of independent retail outlets and six times that of manufacturers' retailers. Also, the sales per square meter are highest in department stores; they are lowest for manufacturers' retailers and regular independent stores. Table 2.16 presents additional dimensions of comparison.

How Retailers are Adapting to Change

Because of the predominance of extremely small establishments in the Japanese retailing sector, it is highly relevant to examine how they perceive the threats of the rapidly changing environment and how they are attempting to cope with them. One would think that, given their extremely limited resources, they would be particularly vulnerable to the onslaught of aggressive large-scale retailing. Before we undertake our analysis of their adaptive behavior, we must acquaint ourselves with their present behavior patterns, attitudes, and ideologies, because only against this background can we fully appreciate the risks and threats of the innovative forces as perceived by small merchants and their efforts (or lack of them) toward rationalization.

For this purpose we shall present relevant findings of a study sponsored by the Ministry of International Trade and Industry.* The

---

*"A Study of Small-scale Retail Establishments," An Investigation of the Distribution Structure (Tokyo: Ryutsu Mondai Kenkyu Kyokai, 1968), pp. 60-99.

TABLE 2.11

Size of Retail Establishments in Japan
by Number of Employees, 1958-70
(in percentages)

Number of Employees	1958	1964	1970
1- 2	70.0	70.3	64.0
3- 4	21.4	19.2	22.5
5- 9	6.8	7.5	9.6
10-19	1.3	2.0	2.6
20-29	0.3	0.5	0.6
30-49	0.1	0.3	0.4
50 or more	0.1	0.2	0.3

Source: Commercial Census, 1971.

study was designed to investigate the attitude and behavior patterns of selected owners of small shops. It was based on extensive personal interviews of a nationwide sample of 1,426 owners of small retail establishments. For the purpose of this study, a small store was defined as one with no more than one or two persons fully occupied in its management. This is the most comprehensive study conducted to date of the profile of owners of small retail stores in Japan.

Looking first at the general character of these stores, we find that 28 percent had an annual sales volume of less than ¥2 million, or roughly $6,000, and stores with sales volume of less than ¥5 million, or $14,000, accounted for 73 percent of the total. Nearly 80 percent of the stores were established after 1945, and 57 percent were established between 1955 and 1964. In 80 percent of the stores surveyed the store and family living quarters were in the same building, and they were separated only in a very rudimentary way. In roughly 93 percent of the stores surveyed, the owners themselves were mainly responsible for operation of the store; in addition, 60 percent of the respondents stated that their wives were also actively involved in its operation.

Another noteworthy finding is that for a substantial number of respondents the store did not constitute their sole source of income. In fact, about one-third of those interviewed indicated that their revenue from the retail store accounted for less than 60 percent of their total income. Nearly 20 percent reported that the income from the

TABLE 2.12

Size of Retail Establishments in Japan by
Floor Space, 1962-67
(in percentages)

Floor Space (in square meters)*	1962	1967	Change 1962-67
1- 9	15.4	10.4	- 5.0
10-19	38.2	33.8	- 4.4
20-29	22.4	22.3	- 0.1
30-49	15.8	19.8	+ 4.0
50-99	6.3	9.3	+ 3.0
100 or more	1.9	4.4	+ 2.5

*One square meter equals 10.8 square feet.

Source: Commercial Census, 1971.

store represented less than 40 percent of the total. Roughly one-fourth of these stores were operated as a side business by wives while their husbands were employed elsewhere.

The absence of clear-cut separation between the store and living quarters goes beyond the physical setting and is reflected in similar practices in financial matters as well. Over 45 percent of those surveyed indicated that no formal distinction was made between their household budget and financial records of the store. Understandably, only a very loose accounting was kept of the store's operations.

Another extremely interesting finding of this survey was that nearly two-thirds of the stores surveyed derived at least half of their total sales from a rather small group of regular customers with whom the store owners were personally acquainted and who lived in the immediate neighborhood. More than one-third of the stores surveyed obtained as high as 70 percent of their total sales from this group of customers. In 60 percent of the stores these regular customers represented fewer than 100 households; in more than two-thirds of the stores, they represented fewer than 200 households. Moreover, 30 percent of their total sales were usually made after 6:00 p.m. These data clearly point to the fact that small retail stores serve a very limited number of customers and trade heavily on personal relationships and convenience.

TABLE 2.13

Retail Stores by Category, 1970

Number of Employees	Total Retail Stores	Ordinary Retail Stores	Department Stores	Self-Service Stores
Total	1,432,436	1,200,552	349	14,271
1- 2	942,759	817,546	-	1,986
3- 4	305,046	254,366	-	3,119
5- 9	131,184	96,361	-	4,232
10-19	36,560	23,223	-	2,723
20-29	8,260	4,867	-	965
30-49	5,032	2,837	-	685
50-99	2,388	1,065	74	410
100 or more	1,207	287	275	151

Number of Employees	Installment Department Stores	Manufacturers' Retail Stores	Automobile Dealers	Gasoline Stations
Total	45,128	131,821	13,153	27,162
1- 2	24,754	89,775	3,023	5,675
3- 4	10,436	27,733	3,901	6,491
5- 9	5,966	10,505	3,264	10,846
10-19	2,491	2,837	1,833	3,453
20-29	799	538	665	426
30-49	428	289	606	187
50-99	187	114	472	66
100 or more	67	30	389	8

Source: Commercial Census, 1971.

These are some of the salient characteristics of the very small retail establishments that still dominate the Japanese distribution scene. They are also characteristic of small stores typically found in almost every part of the world. The survey then inquired into how respondents perceived a series of new developments in the retail field.

The majority of the respondents were aware of growing competitive pressure from other retail establishments. As the most serious source of competition, 28 percent of the respondents cited stores of

TABLE 2.14

Retail Sales by Type of Store, 1970
(in millions of yen)

Number of Employees	Total Retail Stores	Ordinary Retail Stores	Department Stores	Self-Service Stores
Total	16,507,258	9,990,078	1,352,203	1,246,374
1- 2	2,798,513	2,473,963	-	15,366
3- 4	3,061,793	2,621,392	-	51,494
5- 9	3,406,308	2,428,120	-	156,671
10-19	2,112,838	1,211,352	-	239,464
20-29	848,169	402,863	-	162,309
30-49	908,328	355,601	-	203,439
50-99	932,262	252,993	34,915	229,573
100 or more	2,439,049	243,798	1,317,288	188,058

Number of Employees	Installment Department Stores	Manufacturers' Retail Stores	Automobile Dealers	Gasoline Stations
Total	763,905	531,336	1,525,334	1,098,028
1- 2	105,741	143,065	20,158	40,220
3- 4	114,006	116,447	40,906	117,548
5- 9	157,816	112,677	110,464	440,560
10-19	120,027	75,554	168,640	297,801
20-29	58,987	27,341	124,210	72,459
30-49	57,705	23,290	195,905	72,388
50-99	57,610	19,377	287,729	50,967
100 or more	92,013	13,585	577,322	6,985

<u>Source</u>: Commercial Census, 1971.

similar size, 23 percent mentioned stores that are considerably larger than their own, and 30 percent singled out supermarkets. Roughly 20 percent of the respondents, however, felt that they were virtually unaffected by competition. Asked what they feared most from their main competitors, respondents most frequently mentioned wide assortment of merchandise, low price, liberal use of loss leaders, and aggressive promotion.

TABLE 2.15

Annual Sales per Salesperson and per Square
Meter of Sales Space by Categories of Stores, 1970
(in ¥10,000)

Number of Employees	Ordinary Retail Stores	Department Stores	Self-Service Stores	Installment Stores	Manufacturers' Retail Stores
Sales per Salesperson					
All	297	863	710	371	142
1- 2	193	-	430	257	100
3- 4	309	-	474	326	126
5- 9	409	-	562	416	171
10-19	404	-	656	361	206
20-29	351	-	709	313	215
30-49	337	-	792	365	221
50-99	362	690	815	456	249
100 or more	512	869	845	802	271
*Sales per Square Meter**					
All	27.7	48.7	38.4	36.2	15.8
1- 2	14.8	-	17.1	17.7	8.1
3- 4	29.2	-	22.2	21.0	14.8
5- 9	42.2	-	29.2	45.0	24.0
10-19	51.8	-	34.9	54.1	36.0
20-29	50.2	-	39.3	61.4	44.8
30-49	48.4	-	44.8	53.9	56.8
50-99	55.1	37.1	45.7	57.6	84.2
100 or more	72.6	49.1	57.3	96.9	226.4

*One square meter equals 10.8 square feet.

Source: Commercial Census, 1971.

Those who felt that they were competitively vulnerable were asked how they could respond most effectively to this threat. As their single most important tool, over 38 percent of the respondents mentioned greater emphasis on personal service and strengthening personal ties with their customers. Given their traditional background and the absence of other effective competitive tools, this reaction is

TABLE 2.16

Sales Space per Employee and
Stock Turnover by Type of Store, 1970

Sales Space per Employee (in square meters)*

Number of Employees	Total	Ordinary Retail Stores	Department Stores	Self-Service Stores	Installment Stores
All	14.2	10.7	17.7	18.3	10.4
1- 2	15.0	13.0	-	26.6	15.3
3- 4	12.4	10.6	-	21.3	16.3
5- 9	12.0	9.7	-	19.2	11.8
10-19	11.5	7.8	-	18.8	9.9
20-29	12.0	7.0	-	18.0	9.9
30-49	12.7	7.0	-	17.7	10.5
50-99	16.9	6.6	18.5	17.8	8.3
100 or more	17.3	7.1	17.7	14.7	4.8

Stock Turnover

Number of Employees	Total	Ordinary Retail Stores	Department Stores	Self-Service Stores	Installment Stores
All	8.8	8.2	12.2	13.4	7.4
1- 2	7.6	7.6	-	8.7	5.0
3- 4	8.3	8.4	-	10.0	5.8
5- 9	8.3	8.2	-	11.3	7.0
10-19	8.8	8.1	-	13.9	8.3
20-29	10.3	9.0	-	15.1	10.3
30-49	10.3	9.0	-	14.2	8.4
50-99	11.2	9.8	12.3	13.2	9.5
100 or more	12.2	10.0	12.2	15.0	13.5

*One square meter equals 10.8 square feet.

Source: Commercial Census, 1971.

readily understandable. It is extremely interesting to note, however, that nearly 30 percent of respondents felt that there was no effective competitive tool available.

As to the future, those participating in the survey singled out three problem areas as their major sources of concern: (1) profit squeeze, largely resulting from increasing labor cost; (2) intensified competitive pressure; and (3) changes in store patronage patterns and shopping habits of average consumers, particularly their growing preference for one-stop shopping. Despite these problem areas, the study revealed that the majority of respondents were somewhat optimistic about the future. When they were asked about their prospects five years hence, only 28 percent of the respondents had a rather dim view of the future; 43 percent foresaw no significant change; and 26 percent felt that the performance of their stores would improve significantly.

Furthermore, it is significant that 62 percent of the respondents interviewed indicated that they had no specific plans for the future. Twenty-two percent were planning to expand their operations, while only 7 percent were considering either quitting or reducing the size of their operations. The widespread absence of specific plans for the future may well be due partially to the fact that in 41 percent of the stores surveyed, the owner was fifty years old or older. If all owners over forty are included, the proportion goes up to over 70 percent. It is not unreasonable to assume that the age factor is an important variable in determining their attitude toward innovation.

An interesting finding of this survey was that only slightly over half of the respondents had used cash wholesalers, despite the fact that this might have been a readily accessible means of obtaining goods at lower cost, thus enhancing their competitive capacity. The reasons cited for their reluctance to deal with cash wholesalers furnish telling evidence about their attitudes. Of those not buying from cash wholesalers 52 percent (or over 21 percent of the total retailers studied) gave as the most important reason their long-standing and well-established personal relationships with their service wholesalers. These retailers felt a strong sense of obligation to their wholesalers whom they had dealt with for many years, despite the loss of immediate advantages. Thus, personal relationships were shown to be a key factor in retailers' dealings with both their customers and suppliers.

Two dominant characteristics emerge from this study. One is the owners' complacent attitude in the face of the rapidly changing environment. Underlying their lack of a sense of urgency are several major factors. One detects a sense of resignation stemming from their pragmatic experiences—they feel that because they have such limited resources, they could not influence the course of events to any degree no matter how hard they tried. There is also a widely shared view that somehow they could continue to survive despite the changing environment. This stems in part from their intuitive feeling that changes will not take place at as drastic a rate as others anticipate, and that there will always be a demand for their services. Surely, they do concede that some very marginal stores will be forced out by competitive pressure, but they believe that somehow their particular stores will be spared.

Their complacency stems at least in part from the age factor mentioned earlier, which limits their time horizon and alternative opportunities. They are relatively confident that their stores can continue to survive for another five, ten, or even fifteen years. The potential reward for innovation holds little appeal to these men, considering the effort, cost, and risks involved. Moreover, as we have noted, to a substantial number the revenue derived from their stores represents only a supplementary source of income. This fact, too, discourages risk-taking and vigorous effort.

The dominant impression that emerges from this study is that the majority of owners of small retail establishments are vaguely aware of the growing competitive pressure from innovative forces in the distribution system, but despite some exceptions the prevailing mood is that of fatalism. Their defensive actions have been largely limited to improvement of personal services and an attempt to adopt a distinctive merchandising policy.

CHAPTER

3

LARGE-SCALE RETAIL ENTERPRISES

Until rather recently, as we have seen, the retailing sector except for a handful of department stores, was all but dominated by small-scale family establishments. In recent years, however, a number of new types of large-scale retail establishments have emerged to supplement the traditional department stores. These are mass merchandising firms—the Japanese version of supermarkets and discount stores—installment department stores, and chains of specialty stores featuring home appliances, cameras, watches, shoes, and even books.

EMERGENCE OF MASS MERCHANDISING FIRMS

The rise of large-scale mass merchandising firms is phenomenal. As late as 1960 there were but 31 retailing firms whose annual sales volume exceeded ¥5 billion (roughly $14 million) and all but one were traditional department stores. By 1971 there were 101 retail firms with sales of at least ¥6.5 billion. These firms had an aggregate sales volume of slightly over ¥3 trillion, or over 17 percent of total retail sales. The fact that only 101 firms out of 1.4 million establishments accounted for such a high proportion of total sales is very significant, particularly when most of the large firms were of a type new to Japan.

Even more important is the fact that the percentage of total retail sales made by these very large firms has increased from 13.4 percent in 1969, to 14.6 percent in 1970, to more than 17 percent in 1971. Moreover, the twenty largest retail outlets are responsible for almost 60 percent of the total sales reported by the 101 firms.

Turning our attention now to the 100 largest mass merchandising firms in 1971, let us consider some indicators of their size and their increase in a single year, 1970 to 1971. The number of stores controlled by the 100 largest firms increased from 1806 to 2109, and the number of employees from nearly 94,500 to over 116,600. The large increase in total sales and sales per store is also shown in Table 3.1.

Mass merchandising firms, known by such names as supermarkets or superstores, possess characteristics that are commonly associated with American supermarkets and discount stores. They carry a large variety of standard, fast-moving merchandise, and emphasize a merchandising concept of high volume and low margin. Some concentrate on foods and related items, while others have a much wider assortment, including soft goods, household items, sundry goods, cosmetics and drugs, as well as consumer durables.

To illustrate the rapid growth achieved by mass merchandising firms, let us examine the case of Daiei, the largest supermarket chain in Japan. This fantastic story begins in 1951, when Isao Nakauchi opened his first drugstore. The store was no larger than 60 square feet and was a typical small retail store. In 1957, he opened his first self-service store on a very modest scale with merchandise consisting of drugs, cosmetics, and related items. This store was about 1,000 square feet, with only three employees and an annual sales volume of $55,000. By 1971, Daiei had become the largest retail establishment in Japan, with annual sales of roughly $600 million and with 74 stores employing 12,000 people.

Reasons for Rapid Growth

Let us consider briefly what may have accounted for the rapid growth of such mass merchandising firms. The single most important factor is the rapid growth of a mass consumer market. As we have seen, a large number of consumers have suddenly reached a position where they have begun to enjoy some discretionary income. With it, of course, their expectations have risen. Those who have struggled for so long to eke out a bare daily existence now have a chance to improve the quality of their lives.

In order to capture a share of this growing market, large manufacturers introduced new products at a rapid rate and pursued aggressive advertising programs to obtain a larger share of the consumer income. Consumers have been confronted with alternative ways to spend their growing, but still limited, income; their wants have been stimulated, and their consumption horizon has been pushed beyond their available means.

Thus, price has become an extremely important consideration for consumers. Until recently, traditional and conservatively managed

TABLE 3.1

Key Indicators of the 100 Largest
Mass Merchandising Firms, 1971

Year	Number of Stores	Total Sales (¥ million)	Sales per Store (¥ million)	Total Sales Space (in square meters*)	Number of Employees
1970	1,806	1,414,992	783.5	2,882,908	94,462
1971	2,109	1,949,822	924.5	3,694,826	116,609

*One square meter equals 10.8 square feet.

Source: Textile Research Institute, 1972.

department stores had been unable to respond to the new needs of an emerging mass market. These unfulfilled new consumer needs were the very opportunities that mass merchandising firms capitalized on. Aggressive merchandising techniques—strong price appeal, use of price leaders, active advertising and promotion efforts, and limited service—were indeed consonant with the equally aggressive desire of a rising middle class to improve its standard of living.

Through large-volume purchases of well-selected, mass produced, standardized merchandise, and through limited service, these mass merchandising stores have been able to achieve substantial savings, at least part of which are passed on to consumers in lower prices.

Another factor that cannot be ignored is the aggressive entry of large manufacturing firms into the consumer field. Not only can these firms supply large quantities of merchandise of consistent quality, but their strong national brand image, supported by active consumer advertising, has greatly facilitated the growth of mass merchandising.

Still another factor is the trend toward urbanization noted earlier. With urbanization came the rapid growth of suburban towns and satellite cities, offering new market opportunities. In fact, such a market consists primarily of the rising middle class. Mass merchandising firms have been quick to capitalize on the rapid emergence of suburban populations by opening new stores in these areas. This aggressive expansion policy of creating stores where the market is, or is likely to develop, has been another key factor in their success.

TABLE 3.2

Total Purchases Made at Supermarkets for
Selected Food Products, 1971
(in percentages)

Soup cubes	70.4	Canned fish	59.4
Ketchup	64.5	Canned meat	51.7
Mayonnaise	69.4	Instant coffee	72.8
Butter	66.0	Chocolate	51.5
Cheese	67.0	Biscuits & crackers	53.0
Salad oil	51.6	Cake mix	80.3
Canned fruits	63.6	Instant pudding	82.0

Source: Textile Research Institute, 1972.

Traditional department stores, regulated by the Department Store Law, have been seriously handicapped in opening new branch stores.

Kinds of Products Sold

Obviously, the relative importance of supermarkets varies widely among various categories of merchandise. In some merchandise lines the supermarket has become the most important outlet. These items are inexpensively packaged mass consumer goods. Tables 3.2 and 3.3 list a number of products most commonly sold at supermarkets.

Supermarkets are responsible for about a quarter of the total retail sales of soft goods, and for 10 percent of the total sales of foods. In 1971, it is estimated that supermarkets sold about ¥66 billion worth of home appliances, ¥21 billion worth of drugs, and ¥41 billion worth of cosmetics. A comparison of the sales of these and other products by mass merchandising firms and department stores is presented in Table 3.4.

The Entrepreneurs of Mass Merchandising

The significant feature of the rapid rise of the mass merchandising firm is the background of the entrepreneurs who were able to see the profit potentials in the rapidly changing environment and were willing to take the risks in challenging the unknown. Who were this handful of men who broke away from Japanese tradition?

TABLE 3.3

Total Purchases Made at Supermarkets for
Selected Nonfood Products, 1971
(in percentages)

Detergents	35.3
Household cleaners	47.6
Hair oil	23.7
Shampoo	43.9
Toothpaste	52.0
Toilet soap	37.6
Laundry starch	43.9

Source: Textile Research Institute, 1972.

TABLE 3.4

Estimated Total Sales of Selected Key Product
Categories Sold by Mass Merchandising Firms
and Department Stores, 1971
(in millions of yen)

Product	Supermarkets	Department Stores
Soft goods	919,200	764,500
Foods	674,000	320,700
Home appliances	65,900	59,100
Pharmaceuticals	21,200	7,500
Cosmetics	40,700	36,400
Furniture	16,300	94,500
Restaurant services	56,100	83,500

Source: Textile Research Institute, 1972.

Interestingly, the great majority of them came from the retailing sector itself. With few exceptions, however, these men came from outside the established power structure, and their personal backgrounds vary considerably. Some were the owners of small independent retail stores; others entered retailing simply to eke out a living in the immediate aftermath of World War II. Some inherited their small stores. Some were born and raised in relatively affluent families and had the benefits of higher education, but others had barely finished elementary school. They are relatively young men, at least according to Japanese standards. The majority belong to the generation most severely affected by the war.

While their backgrounds differ, two characteristics stand out. One is that they usually do not share the social and educational characteristics of the elite; the second is that their backgrounds vary in other ways as well, presenting a dramatic contrast to the homogeneity of the professional managerial class that dominates large industrial and financial corporations in Japan.

Japan's large-scale retail firms fall into four basic categories: department stores, supermarket chains, installment credit stores, and chains of specialty stores featuring relatively standardized products such as home appliances, shoes, and certain types of apparel. Beginning with supermarket chains, we shall examine each of the four different types of large-scale retail institutions.

SUPERMARKET CHAINS

Let us now turn to an examination of salient operating characteristics of the new supermarket chains. Here we shall draw heavily upon a recent study undertaken by the Textile Research Institute. This study is an in-depth examination of the 100 largest supermarket chains in Japan. The profile of these 100 chains will afford an excellent picture of supermarket chains in Japan. These large chains are becoming increasingly important: their share of the total sales by all supermarkets increased from 55 percent in 1969 to 82 percent in 1971.

Looking at further data on these 100 mass merchandising firms, we should note that 48 of the 100 chains had an annual sales volume ranging from ¥2 billion to ¥6 billion. Another 26 had annual sales of from ¥6 to ¥10 billion. Thus, 74 of the 100 largest chains had a sales volume of less than ¥10 billion. Among the remaining 26, 14 had sales of at least ¥20 billion, and 7 had sales of ¥50 billion or more.

Trend Toward Greater Concentration

A notable trend among these supermarket chains is that greater concentration is now taking place among the larger firms. We just noted that the 100 largest chains are responsible for 82 percent of the total sales by all supermarkets; moreover, the ten largest of these account for 58 percent of the total sales reported by the 100 chains. These and other details are presented in Table 3.5. Table 3.6 names the ten largest supermarket chains ranked by their 1971 sales volume. These ten firms have achieved substantial growth over the past decade.

TABLE 3.5

Concentration of Supermarket Sales
Among the Large Firms, 1971
(in billions of Yen and percentages)

Value of Sales	
Total retail sales	17,688.4
Total supermarket sales	2,390.0
Sales by the 100 largest supermarket chains	1,955.8
Sales by the 10 largest supermarket chains	1,134.6
Percentages	
Total supermarket sales / Total retail sales	13.5
Sales by 100 largest chains / Total retail sales	11.1
Sales of 100 largest chains / Sales of all supermarkets	81.8
Sales of the 10 largest chains / Total retail sales	6.4
Sales by 10 largest chains / Sales by 100 largest chains	58.0
Supermarket sales, 1970/1971	119.5
Sales of the 100 largest supermarket chains, 1970/1971	138.2
Sales of the 10 largest supermarket chains, 1970/1971	148.6

Source: Textile Research Institute, 1972.

TABLE 3.6

The Ten Largest Supermarket Chains
in Japan Ranked by Sales, 1971

Name of Firm	Annual Sales (in square meters)	Number of Stores	Floor Space
Daiei	14,289	58	231,326
Seiyu	12,000	83	180,111
Jasco	9,590	76	157,080
Yuni	8,500	103	253,212
Nichi Ichi Chain	8,000	109	166,544
Nagasakiya	5,806	66	244,837
Ito Yoka	5,000	23	80,100
Tsuchigami Yanido Fuchigami	5,000	20	94,790
Izumiya	4,201	38	120,070
Toko	4,000	48	50,313

Source: Textile Research Institute, 1972.

The 100 largest chains are responsible for 67.5 percent of the total sales of soft goods by all supermarkets, the ten largest chains alone accounting for over 61 percent. In home appliances, the 100 largest chains sell 73 percent of the total sales by all supermarkets; nearly 76 percent of these sales are handled by the ten largest chains. Similarly, the 100 largest firms are responsible for 75 percent and 71 percent of the total sales of pharmaceuticals and cosmetics, respectively, by all supermarkets. Of these, roughly 49 percent and 70 percent, respectively, are sold by the ten largest chains.

Diversity of Product Lines

A distinguishing characteristic of the Japanese version of supermarket chains is the very diversity of their merchandise lines. Basically, according to their origin, there are two categories of supermarkets existing in Japan. One type originated as food stores; the other is made up of those which developed from stores specializing in apparel. Table 3.7 presents the types of merchandise carried by each category of supermarket. Both types of stores have been widening their lines of merchandise and, in some cases, they have become almost indistinguishable.

TABLE 3.7

Major Merchandise Categories of Japanese
Supermarket Chains, 1971
(in percentages)

	Food-oriented Supermarkets	Nonfood-oriented Supermarkets
Foods	62.8	26.1
Apparel	14.9	52.0
Pharmaceuticals	1.3	1.0
Cosmetics	2.6	1.9
Home appliances	1.9	3.9
Other sundry items	13.5	10.9
Restaurants and other services	3.0	2.8
	100.0	100.0

Source: Textile Research Institute, 1972.

Financial Ratios

Let us now examine the financial statistics of the 100 largest supermarket chains. Table 3.8 presents in a summary form the average performance of the firms surveyed for 1968 and 1971, with key financial ratios. As is typically the case in Japan, these supermarket chains have relied heavily on debt sources to finance their expansion. For example, according to this study, during the fiscal year 1971, the eighteen largest chains for which the data were obtained spent, in the aggregate, a total of roughly ¥53 billion for capital investment. Of this amount, 57 percent was externally financed. Of the total debt, roughly 95 percent was obtained through loans from private financial institutions.

To illustrate the operating characteristics and performances of larger supermarket chains, Table 3.9 presents key operating ratios of Daiei, the largest chain in Japan.

In addition to supermarket chains, there are two other noteworthy mass merchandising institutions in Japan that are quickly gaining a foothold. They are installment credit stores, the so-called "credit department stores," and the chains of specialty shops featuring one major merchandise category. We shall briefly examine salient operating characteristics of each type.

TABLE 3.8

Average Key Financial Ratios of the 100 Largest
Supermarket Chains, 1968 and 1971
(in percentages)

	1968	1971
Current assets/Current liabilities	105.0	73.8
Total equity/Total assets	20.1	12.8
Total debts/Total equity	150.8	327.3
Profits before taxes/Sales	3.0	2.6
Cost of goods sold/Accounts & notes payable	4.6	3.6
Net profit/Total assets	4.0	2.1
Net profit/Equity	19.9	16.3
Total operating expenses/Net profit	79.4	81.2
Interest charges/Net sales	1.3	2.8
Gross profit/Sales	19.7	23.7

Source: Textile Research Institute, 1972.

TABLE 3.9

Key Operating Ratios, Daiei
Chain, 1971

Total sales/Equity	19.2%
Total sales/Fixed assets	3.1
Fixed assets/Equity	614.3
Current assets/Current liabilities	93.6
Equity/Total assets	10.2
Debts/Equity	631.7
Net profit after tax/Total sales	1.1
Net profit/Total sales	16.3
Net profit after tax/Total assets	2.2
Net profit after tax/Equity	21.5
Interest paid/Total sales	2.0

Source: Textile Research Institute.

INSTALLMENT CREDIT STORES

Altogether, it is estimated that there are 11,000 installment stores in Japan. Among the 100 largest mass merchandising firms, however, there are only four "credit department stores," a unique marketing institution developed in Japan. Among these Marui, the largest, had annual sales close to ¥50 billion in 1971 and Midoriya, the second largest, recorded annual sales of ¥45 billion in that year. Marui was established prior to the war, but its major growth has taken place in the past decade or so. It has been largely instrumental in introducing the new concept of installment sales into Japan. The company has followed an aggressive growth policy and by 1971 it had 29 stores employing 4,600 persons.

The success of these firms can be attributed to their ability to introduce a new image for credit purchases. The consumer image of installment sales had been rather negative until recently, and merchandise of inferior quality had been associated with questionable sales practices. Leading installment department stores have now been able to overcome this image. They have made particularly intensive efforts to cultivate youth, both single and married, and have tailored their merchandising policy to meet the needs and aspirations of the young.

Typically, these very large installment department stores carry a wide assortment of merchandise. In terms of the breadth of merchandise carried, they are hardly distinguishable from regular full-fledged department stores. These stores sell for cash as well as for credit, different prices being charged for the same merchandise. Credit sales typically require a 10 percent down payment, and the balance is paid in nine monthly installments. The maximum length of credit is ordinarily ten months.

SPECIALTY CHAIN STORES

The development of chains among certain types of specialty stores is also noteworthy. Among the 100 largest retail firms, there are twelve firms which can be classified in this category. Among these firms, all but two are geared to the mass market. In terms of merchandise, there are five in home appliances, two in books, two in shoes, two in apparel, and one in pharmaceuticals.

In comparison with other large-scale retailing firms, they are relatively small. The average annual sales are slightly more than ¥10 billion, or roughly one-third of the average reported by other types of large-scale firms. The largest specialty store ranks 36th in the top 100, with total sales of ¥24.5 billion; the total sales of all twelve firms of this type account for less than 5 percent of the total sales of the top 100. Although these firms are relatively small, they have achieved a very rapid growth rate over the past several years, averaging around 33 percent per annum, in contrast to 17 percent and 20 percent for department stores and supermarket chains, respectively.

TRADITIONAL MARKETING INSTITUTIONS

Although the mass merchandising field is now largely dominated by aggressive entrepreneurs who rose rapidly from obscurity, it is not their exclusive domain. Old-line establishments have been actively seeking opportunities in this rapidly growing field. Particularly notable are the department stores that are owned and managed by a number of private railroad companies and located near large cities, particularly Tokyo. These railroads service Tokyo's rapidly growing suburbs. The companies have built department stores at the major railroad terminals, and more recently they have gone into mass merchandising operations. Taking further advantage of their strategic positions, they have recently diversified into real estate development, sightseeing, bus lines, taxis, and other related transportation and service businesses.

These urban railroad-based conglomerates enjoy several advantages in entering the large-scale mass merchandising field: (1) extensive land ownership along their railroad lines is extremely valuable for store sites; (2) they can locate their stores as a part of planned housing developments, and thus have a clear advantage over competitors in the choice of store locations; and (3) they often have greater access to managerial and financial resources, including good banking connections. A most successful example of mass merchandising operations of this type is the Seiyu chain, part of the Seibu Railroad group, which is now the second-largest mass merchandising firm in Japan.

In addition, there are three other powerful groups that are eyeing the mass merchandising field with increasing interest. The traditional department stores that until recently had adhered to their own merchandising philosophy have now become increasingly intrigued by rapidly growing opportunities in mass merchandising, and a number of prestigious department stores have diversified into such operations. Also, large trading firms have become increasingly active in this field. We shall further examine the activities of these trading companies in Chapter 5.

There is yet another type of institution that has considerable interest in entry into the mass merchandising field. These are cooperatives of both the consumer and agricultural types. Consumer cooperatives in Japan, despite their long history, have not been fully developed. It is estimated that there are some 1,600 consumer cooperatives with approximately 8 million members and total annual sales of around ¥150 billion. Most of these stores are still rather small. There are some exceptions, however. For example, several cooperative-sponsored chains are included among the 100 largest chains. The largest of these is the Nada Kobe supermarket, which boasted annual sales of ¥24 billion in the fiscal year ending in March 1969. This chain has 27 stores in eight major cities in the Osaka-Kobe area, serving some 160,000 member households. Its sales experienced a fifteenfold growth in the decade ending in 1969. Many consumer cooperatives are now making concerted efforts to develop along the lines of the Nada Kobe chain.

Much more powerful than consumer cooperatives are the agricultural cooperatives. There are roughly 7,000 agricultural cooperatives located throughout Japan, with a total membership of some 5 million agricultural households. The annual volume of purchasing done through the central purchasing unit of the Agricultural Cooperative Federation exceeds ¥740 billion; the goods purchased are distributed through their diverse cooperative organizations. One of the important services that the agricultural cooperatives provide is retail outlets for daily necessities. More than 4,200 cooperatives maintain altogether nearly 10,000 outlets of this type for their membership, with total sales of some ¥160 billion. Out of these 10,000 outlets, roughly 3,000 are self-service stores.

At present over 90 percent of these stores are small, with less than 230 square meters (roughly 2,500 square feet) of sales space. But they can become a very potent force in the large-scale retail operation field because they enjoy several unique advantages. They already have a powerful central buying organization that can be readily mobilized. They can rely on the active support of their membership and they also have relatively abundant financial resources. There is growing evidence that agricultural cooperatives are expanding rapidly and are already posing a serious competitive threat to regular supermarket chains.

IMPLICATIONS AND FUTURE PROSPECTS FOR RETAILING

The emergence of large-scale mass merchandising firms in Japan is indeed a very recent phenomenon, but already this development has had a far-reaching impact and is altering the basic structure of the Japanese distribution system. In this section we shall examine major implications of this development and discuss the prospects for the future. First, the rapid rise of large-scale innovative mass merchandising firms has resulted in the emergence of an entirely new method of distributing mass-produced standard merchandise, providing a new alternative to both manufacturers and consumers. Second, the rapidly growing mass merchandising establishments have given rise to what Palamountain calls vertical conflict, that is, struggle between different levels of the distribution channel*, particularly between large oligopolistic manufacturers and large-scale mass merchandisers.

During the last decade or so, the initiative in and control over distribution of a number of key consumer products has shifted from dominant wholesalers to large manufacturers. Indeed, in mass produced and nationally advertised products, large oligopolistic manufacturers have now assumed the leadership role in the distribution channels. Traditionally, because of their very small size, the power of retailers has been very limited; but now mass merchandising firms are challenging the existing power structure.

We have observed that in certain processed food items, the self-service outlets account for more than 50 percent of total sales. Likewise, in certain standard apparel lines they are responsible for an important share. For example, for fiscal year 1968, the 100 largest chains sold over ¥383.3 billion (over $1 billion) worth of apparel. Jasco, the largest chain in the soft goods line, is reported to have sold 870,000 dress shirts, 1.7 million women's blouses, 1.8 million women's sweaters, 2.1 million slips, 7.9 million pairs of stockings, and more than 4.5 million pairs of men's socks during the same year.† In the home appliance field, mass merchandising firms in the aggregate account for less than 2 percent of the total sales of those products; however, sales by a few leading firms are of significant size. For example, during fiscal year 1968 Daiei sold some ¥6 billion worth of home appliances, and for 1969 about ¥10 billion worth. Seiyu, the largest chain, sold ¥3 billion worth of home appliances in 1968 and around ¥5 billion worth in 1969.

The Power Struggle in Distribution

Fully aware of their newly gained strength, which is rapidly increasing, mass merchandising firms have now begun to exert their

---

*Joseph C. Palamountain, Jr., The Politics of Distribution (Cambridge, Mass.: Harvard University Press, 1955), p. 48.

†A Report on Operating Characteristics of 100 Chains (Tokyo: Nihon Sen-I-Kenkyūjo, 1969), pp. 37-41.

power in several ways. First, these firms have now grown to a point at which large manufacturers of many consumer products can hardly ignore them as an important outlet for their products. Mass merchandising firms initially experienced considerable difficulty in buying national brands, at least through legitimate sources; but generally this condition no longer exists. These firms have now gained a sufficient degree of consumer acceptance to accord them a powerful voice in their dealings with manufacturers.

The reactions of large manufacturers to mass merchandising firms have varied widely. A relatively small number of manufacturers steadfastly have refused to sell to these firms for fear of antagonizing their existing customers. Some manufacturing firms are ambivalent. This is reflected in their policy of not actively soliciting sales to mass merchandising firms, but yet being relatively lax in policing if their products find their way onto the counters of these firms.

An increasing number of manufacturing firms, however, view the growing power of mass merchandising firms as the wave of the future, and they are actively seeking business from these establishments. As a result, with a few notable exceptions, the newly emerging mass merchandising firms can now buy whatever they desire from almost any sources at their own terms. Not only do they enjoy access to a wide variety of the well-known national brands but also considerable freedom in determining at what price products can be sold to consumers. Pleas by major manufacturers to adhere to their suggested prices have often gone unheeded, and national brands have been widely used as loss leaders by supermarket and discount chains to entice customers to their stores.

A very interesting trend that began to emerge in late 1969 was a perceptible change in the attitude of major manufacturers of home appliances toward mass merchandising firms. Until recently their policy was characterized as one of reluctant acquiescence. The official posture of these manufacturers was to refuse to sell to mass merchandising firms, particularly to those that were not willing to conform to the manufacturers' suggested retail prices. As a result, the mass merchandising firms had to obtain their inventory from irregular sources. They experienced little difficulty in doing so. Recognizing the growing importance of mass merchandising firms, however, several major manufacturers have taken the initiative in setting up special outlets to supply them, sometimes in the form of special subsidiaries. Thus, even hitherto most reluctant home appliance manufacturers began to recognize the inevitability of having to "normalize" their relationship with mass merchandisers. The mass retailers were, of course, faced with the need to increase their home appliance sales in order to assure sufficient quantities of merchandise. To do so, in many cases they had to agree to conform to the minimum price suggested by the manufacturers. In this respect, the current development represents a pragmatic compromise between the two.

In a number of product categories, mass merchandising firms are now attempting to bypass wholesalers and to deal directly with large manufacturers. In some cases mass merchandising firms have been forced to purchase directly from manufacturers from sheer necessity, since wholesalers often are not capable of supplying the large demands of the mass merchandising firms. In certain limited product lines, large-scale mass merchandising firms can now generate a sufficient volume to demand direct purchase from large manufacturers. The most immediate advantage to the chains is, of course, the lower price that gives them a competitive edge over their smaller competitors. It also opens up an entirely new horizon to retailers, such as having large well-known manufacturers produce specially designed merchandise, thus paving the way to the adoption of a private brand policy.

Thus, some large mass merchandising firms have now gone into private branding. In these instances the large mass merchandising firms work closely with wholesalers or directly with manufacturers. This approach has several well-known advantages, such as avoiding direct price competition with national brands and increasing store loyalty. The extent to which private brand practices have been adopted, of course, varies among firms and among product lines within a firm. For example, in one leading firm, 75 percent of the total sales of ladies lingerie, 65 percent of the sales of ladies foundations, and 46 percent of the sales of blouses came from private brands.

Although private brand merchandise has been most commonly found among high-volume food and apparel items, a few large mass merchandising firms have now begun to extend this practice to selected home appliances. This is particularly significant, inasmuch as the home appliance industry has been known for the dominant role occupied by large manufacturers in the distribution structure. In 1971, Daei took control of a medium-size consumer electronics manufacturing firm to create a captive supply of home appliances. Color television sets were sold at a drastic discount price, creating a sensation in the market place.

To develop their unique merchandise lines, some of the large retail chains have now established product-planning groups and have strengthened the functions of merchandising managers. Some have incorporated separate subsidiaries for this purpose. These subsidiaries, or satellite firms as they are often called, are frequently financed jointly by wholesalers and manufacturers who are interested in supplying these chains.

The development of private brands, though still in the formative stage, is significant evidence of the growing power of large-scale mass merchandising firms. A recent survey of supermarkets in Tokyo revealed that 36 percent of 376 participating firms indicated that they were selling some merchandise under their own brands. Products that are sold most frequently under private brands include soup, canned fruits, cooking oil, instant coffee, men's socks, dress shirts, sheets, women's blouses, stockings, and underwear.

Large chains follow two different strategies in this regard. One is to persuade large manufacturers with well-known national brands to manufacture private brand merchandise. This is being done in some of the processed food items, such as mayonnaise. For understandable reasons, large manufacturers are ambivalent about entering into private branding; as a result (though there are a few notable exceptions), this practice has not yet gained wide acceptance. It is true, however, that large manufacturers of selected consumers' goods are coming under growing pressure from large chains, and no doubt this will be one of the most important marketing decisions they must make in the next few years. Indeed, "the battle of the brands," a struggle so familiar on the American distribution scene, has already begun in Japan.

A rather unique and noteworthy compromise has evolved out of this "battle of the brands" between large manufacturers and large chains. This is the use of "dual brands," as they have become known in Japan; that is, offering merchandise bearing both the manufacturer's and the retailer's brand name. The practice has proved to be advantageous both to chains and to major manufacturers of national brands. Retailers can benefit from the prestige associated with the manufacturer's brand name as well as from their own promotional efforts. For example, the Seiyu chain has recently begun to sell salad oil under the dual brand names of Seiyu and Mitsubishi Trading Company. A major theme in their promotion is "Mitsubishi quality and Seiyu price." Dual brand names are also more palatable to large manufacturers, who may be unwilling to manufacture private brand merchandise. It is too early to predict at this time whether the practice of dual branding will become a permanent and widespread aspect of the nation's distribution scene.

The second approach followed by mass merchandising firms is to have small manufacturers produce private brand merchandise for them. Given the large number of small manufacturers and the keen competition that exists among them, they are more than willing to supply private brands for large retail chains. Here, however, continued assurance of supply and quality maintenance often present difficult problems.

Some mass merchandising firms have gone a step further by organizing a separate subsidiary to supply certain high-volume standard merchandise to be sold under their brand names. For example, Seiyu now has two separate subsidiaries that supply meat to the Seiyu stores. Some merchandisers have also organized a network of controlled manufacturers. Seiyu, in cooperation with Mitsubishi Trading Company, organized a number of small manufacturers into a centrally coordinated and controlled team to make certain apparel lines. This merchandise is, of course, being sold under Seiyu's private brand name.

Among a number of volatile and dynamic developments now taking place in Japan's distribution scene, particularly significant is the change in the power relationship in the distribution system. As noted earlier, it is only in recent years that large manufacturers in certain industries have emerged as the dominant force in the distribution channel. (These firms have taken the lead in product design and manufacture, as well.) They have generally acted as "captain of the channel." This newly gained power of large manufacturers in the area of marketing is now being challenged by emerging large-scale mass merchandising firms. The latter are anxious to assume many, if not all, of the marketing functions once performed by manufacturers and to claim a greater share of the profit accruing to the performance of such functions. Large manufacturers of consumer goods are aware of these developments and are naturally anxious to retain their power and, of course, the profit associated with such power. It is quite likely, therefore, that the contest between large manufacturers and large-scale mass merchandising firms may intensify.

What does the future hold for large-scale mass merchandising firms? There is a consensus that they will continue to grow. According to one widely accepted projection, total retail sales in Japan will reach ¥52,100 billion by 1980. That is, retail sales will achieve, at least nominally, more than threefold growth in the 1970s. Two examples will illustrate the magnitude of growth these firms are seeking to achieve: the Seibu distribution group is aiming at becoming the nation's largest retail enterprise by 1975, with sales of ¥1 trillion. However, Daiei, currently Japan's largest supermarket chain, is planning to increase its sales to ¥1.15 trillion annually by 1975.

As presented in Table 3.10, the distribution of total retail sales by type of store will undergo considerable change. By the end of this decade, department stores will account for nearly 22 percent of the total sales, and supermarkets, 17 percent. The share of the independent retail outlets is projected to decline to less than 57 percent as contrasted with their 71 percent of a decade earlier.

When analyzed by merchandise categories, by 1975 it is projected that department stores will make slightly over 25 percent of

TABLE 3.10

Projected Retail Sales by Types
of Stores, 1969-80
(in billions of yen and percentages)

Type of Store	1969	1975	1980
Department stores			
Total sales	1,550	4,856	11,345
	11.1	16.9	21.8
Supermarkets			
Total sales	1,670	4,446	8,866
	12.0	15.5	17.0
Independent stores			
Total sales	9,940	17,971	29,472
	71.2	62.6	56.6
Installment stores			
Total sales	320	545	9,390
	2.3	1.9	1.8
Others			
Total sales	480	875	1,462
	3.4	3.1	2.8
Total retail sales	13,960	28,693	52,085
	100	100	100

Source: Textile Research Institute, 1971.

the total textile and apparel sales, and 6.6 percent of food sales. Supermarket chains in 1975 will account for 28 percent and 13 percent, respectively, of these categories. It is significant, however, that although the percentage will decline slightly, independent retail outlets will still account for over three-fourths of total food sales. The details are presented in Table 3.11.

Major Challenges

No doubt, mass merchandising firms will continue to grow at a brisk rate, but at the same time there are a number of major challenges which they must be ready to face. First, these firms will be the subject of greater competitive pressure. This will come from several sources. In the formative stage, mass merchandising firms

TABLE 3.11

Actual and Projected Sales of Merchandise by
Type of Retail Store, 1970 and 1975
(in billions of yen and percentages)

	1970					1975			
	Textiles & Apparel	Food	Other	Total		Textiles & Apparel	Food	Other	Total
Department stores								
Total sales	765	320	779	1,864	1,896	729	2,231	4,856
	20.5	4.8	14.6	11.9	25.5	6.6	21.9	16.9
Supermarkets								
Total sales	919	674	406	1,999	2,100	1,469	877	4,446
	24.6	10.1	7.6	12.7	28.3	13.3	8.6	15.5
Independent stores								
Total sales	1,806	5,500	3,663	10,969	3,049	8,627	6,295	17,971
	48.2	82.8	69.0	69.9	41.1	77.8	61.7	62.6
Installment stores								
Total sales	166	—	177	343	234	—	311	545
	4.5	—	3.3	2.2	3.2	—	3.1	1.9
Others								
Total sales	81	149	295	525	142	252	481	875
	2.2	2.3	5.5	3.3	1.9	2.3	4.7	3.1
Total retail sales	3,737	6,643	5,320	15,700	7,421	11,077	10,195	28,693
	100.0	100.0	100.0	100.0	100.0	100.0	100.0	100.0

Source: Textile Research Institute, 1971.

owed their rapid growth at least in part to the very ineptness of small traditional retail firms. The former had innovative ideas and were able to capitalize on them. The situation, however, has changed radically. In a number of attractive market areas, large retail chains have begun to come into direct competition with one another. Intense competition among giant mass merchandising firms is bidding up already rapidly rising real estate prices in attractive market areas, making the addition of new stores extremely costly. Moreover, competition is being further intensified by increasingly active entry of outside elements into this field. We have already noted the entry of consumer and agricultural cooperatives. In addition, traditional department stores, large trading companies, and real estate development firms are eyeing this field with aggressive interest.

In addition to the external challenges, there are several major problems that are internal to these rapidly growing chains. The most immediate problem is the rapidly increasing capital requirement to finance expansion. Not unlike large manufacturing firms in Japan, to finance their growth large mass merchandising firms have depended heavily on borrowing. As a result, their debt-equity ratio is staggeringly high. Daiei, for example, had been capitalized at only ¥4 million, but this figure has recently been increased to over ¥32 million. Even now, considering the total annual sales of over ¥100 billion, this capitalization is extremely small. The cost of new store sites in attractive market areas, as we have noted, is rapidly increasing. Construction costs are also rising. For example, it is estimated that in 1969 building and equipping a store with roughly 5,000 square feet of floor space in a major metropolitan market would cost at least ¥300 million ($830,000).

In order to realize their goals, large-scale retailing firms must undertake large capital investment at a rapid rate. A survey of planned capital investment for fiscal year 1970 among the 20 leading firms revealed that they were intending to increase their capital investment substantially over the preceding year.* Capital investment planned by these mass merchandising chains for fiscal year 1970 averaged about ¥9.3 billion. New stores being planned are considerably larger and, as a result, more expensive than those built in the past. Significantly, these firms plan to finance at least 70 percent of this capital investment through debt sources. Daiei, for example, is planning to raise nearly 90 percent of ¥25 billion in funds for expansion through borrowing.

---

*"Toward National Chains," <u>Nihon Keizai Shinbun</u>, (January 21, 1970), p. 8.

To obtain additional funds, some firms are now planning to go public. At the same time they are developing close banking connections. Japan's leading city banks, which traditionally had favored large manufacturing firms, have become increasingly interested in developing closer ties with the rapidly growing retail chains. Already some of the major city banks have gone beyond ordinary banking relationships. Several major banks now have their former employees in top management positions in a number of large mass merchandising firms. Some have entered into the store and equipment leasing business through their subsidiaries. Others have collaborated in the development of shopping centers. Growing dependence on the major city banks for funds, however, will likely constrain the freedom of action of these stores. Obtaining necessary funds to finance their ambitious expansion programs undoubtedly will be a major challenge to the management of expansion-oriented large mass merchandising firms.

Even more serious problems lie in the areas of organizational development and management resources. It may be recalled that most of the large-scale mass merchandising firms grew out of small-scale operations in a very short time. These firms have grown under the dynamic and capable leadership of aggressive entrepreneurs, but they have now grown into large enterprises, requiring different types of managerial leadership, styles, and skills.

It is axiomatic that problems associated with managing enterprises with ¥400 billion annual sales are considerably different from those of an enterprise with annual sales of ¥50 billion. Particularly, in order to achieve their ambitious goals, these firms must undertake active diversification programs. A number of large mass merchandising firms have already begun diversifying into such leisure-related service fields as restaurants, hotels, drive-in restaurants, amusement centers, travel services, and sport facilities. A number of mass merchandising firms are now developing into large diversified conglomerates. In this context organizational and managerial development becomes of utmost importance. Development of strategic planning, formulation of well-defined corporate goals and strategies, and establishment of management information and control systems will become urgent.

The top management of large-scale firms now faces a dual challenge of achieving significant growth, on one hand, and at the same time shaping internal organization and a management system that is adequate to meet the increasingly complex demands of growing size and diversity. In meeting these challenges, the most critical factor, of course, is managerial capabilities. The future growth potential of the rapidly emerging chains depends, to a large degree, on whether or not these obviously successful entrepreneurs can transform themselves into capable organizational builders and managers of large-scale and highly complex diversified enterprises.

Another closely related critical issue is whether or not the chief executives of these enterprises can develop successfully an effective and capable top management team. Despite this obvious need, some of the top management positions in these rapidly growing chains are now occupied by men who have been propelled to top positions with the growth of their firms, but who lack the ability and skill to become effective members of the top management team in a large enterprise. They are the ones who shared the difficulty and growing pains in the initial phase of the venture and who were highly effective then; but, unfortunately, unlike some of their better-equipped colleagues, they have outlived their usefulness now that the firm has become extremely large and complex.

Ironically, the very success the firm has achieved, to which these men have contributed significantly, has made their skills, temperament, and background obsolete. This is a tragedy that is commonly observed in firms that have experienced very rapid growth. Understandably, these men often feel that they are now rightful partakers of the fruits of success, and the entrepreneur can hardly be blamed for his personal attachment to them. What to do with these men presents a very serious dilemma to the chief executives of many of the rapidly growing chains, inasmuch as the continued growth and success of these firms depends on the capacity of an effective top management team.

Another closely related problem is the recruitment and development of middle management. The absence of a sufficient number of well-trained middle management personnel will be a major deterrent to growth. Both line managers and staff specialists in large-scale retailing must be developed in sufficient quantity. With the rapid expansion of large-scale mass merchandising firms, a shortage of qualified middle management and staff specialists is becoming increasingly keen. A particularly crucial need is the development of highly skilled and capable merchandising managers. Trained individuals who readily can assume managerial responsibilities in newly emerging chains are indeed scarce. As a result, the burden of development of middle management falls squarely on the firms themselves.

Most of the large-scale mass merchandising firms are now actively recruiting college graduates. For example, Daiei recently recruited some 300 college graduates and Seiyu hired about 100. Retailing has not been a very popular field among college students, but with the emergence of large-scale retailing, the traditional view is undergoing a gradual change. Particularly among graduates of less-prestigious universities who are at a disadvantage in seeking employment with leading Japanese industrial or financial firms, the mass merchandising field provides an attractive alternative. Also appealing to them is the presence of ample opportunity for rapid advancement. The very nature of chain operations requires a certain degree of decentralization, and as a result it demands managers who are willing to assume responsibility. Despite these favorable trends, firms must still find, train, and develop their managers.

Since there are few established patterns to follow, mass merchandising firms are learning on a trial-and-error basis. Of course, the dynamic nature of this industry is a compensating factor, since it does provide a high degree of motivation and ample opportunity to move up in the organization for those willing to assume responsibility. Top management of mass merchandising firms is keenly aware of the importance of managerial recruitment and development; in fact, it is often their greatest concern.

Another critical factor relating to personnel is the growing general labor shortage and accompanying rise in wages. A number of mass merchandising firms, particularly of small and medium size, are experiencing some difficulties in recruiting first-line personnel. Mass merchandising firms operating on low margins are particularly vulnerable to a profit squeeze through rapidly accelerating wage increases. As a result, they are now compelled to rationalize management practices to increase the productivity of each employee.

Closely related to the foregoing is one disturbing attitude that is widely shared by the top management of a number of these mass merchandising firms—their preoccupation with sales volume. Frequently their goals are defined in terms of total sales. Seldom is reference made to such critical measures as profit or return on investment. This emphasis on sales volume is common among Japanese executives, regardless of their industry. The reason for this preoccupation is that sales volume is the most direct and immediate measure of the relative standing of an enterprise. It is the single most effective measure of a firm's growing importance, and it can be used with considerable effectiveness to demonstrate the retailer's newly gained power to outside elements such as manufacturers and wholesalers. While the continued use of this measure may be desirable for external use or public image, for the purpose of internal management planning and control the overemphasis on sales volume is fraught with potential dangers. It tends to bring about cutthroat competition, making profit a secondary concern and generating dangerous pressure to undertake reckless expansion programs merely to meet the sales target. Thus, the top management of many of the mass merchandising firms now needs to reorient its thinking in this regard.

New Strategies

We have briefly discussed major challenges that must be faced by Japan's large-scale mass merchandising firms if they are to achieve their planned goals. In order to meet these challenges and to capitalize on very dynamic growth opportunities, Japan's large-scale retailing firms are mapping out new strategies. Of these, several noteworthy developments are taking shape. One is the already noted trend for diversification, with the goal of developing a widely diversified enterprise centering around retailing. A number of large retailing firms are planning horizontal diversification into such fields as shopping center development, real estate, and housing. They are also entering leisure-related industries, including hotels, restaurants, bowling facilities, sight-seeing, and amusement and recreational centers.

Second, the relationship among large-scale firms is becoming increasingly fluid. As noted earlier, truly intense competition among them has just begun, as each of the large chains pushes its own expansion programs, thus bringing them into direct confrontation with one another. It is extremely interesting that, for mutual advantage, many of these firms are willing to enter into cooperative arrangements of various types, ranging from exchange of information to cooperative buying and even to collaboration in opening new stores.

Particularly significant are several cases of joint action to avoid competition taken by firms when entering into new areas. This trend may well accelerate as the competition becomes more intense and as the attractive new markets become saturated. This approach also enables them to combine their resources and distinctive competence. To cope with the aggressive efforts toward national chains, somewhat smaller regional chains are taking similar actions. For example, in early 1970 seven regional chains formed a joint purchasing subsidiary.

What is most significant in interfirm cooperation among large mass merchandising firms is the flexibility and dynamism they demonstrate in entering into these arrangements. They have little tradition to uphold: if they see mutual advantages in these arrangements, they implement them with little hesitation. It is not difficult to conceive that these cooperative arrangements may well eventually lead to mergers among these firms. As growing competition among mass merchandising firms escalates, and especially with the possibility of entry of large-scale American retailing firms, mergers will undoubtedly occur, particularly among medium-size firms, as their very survival may well become endangered.

The most significant merger up to now is the formation of Jasco in 1969 through the merger of three large regional chains. The combined firm now is the third largest mass merchandising chain in Japan.

The trend toward greater concentration became even more evident in late 1969 as large chains intensified their efforts to become truly national in scope. Daiei, for example, entered into cooperative arrangements with several local chains and also began franchising operations.

We should also note here that the process of elimination already has begun among some of these firms. This is particularly true among small to medium-size companies that find it increasingly difficult to withstand aggressive competition from large-scale chains. Many of these small- to medium-size mass merchandising firms entered this field without adequate planning and resources. It is not unlikely that they will be acquired by large chains as the latter press for expansion.

The last, but not the least important, new strategy is the increasingly closer relationships that are developing between large-scale mass merchandising firms and large trading firms. This move, which began in early 1969, was surprising to many since it was often thought that, to the innovative mass merchandising firms, the trading companies represented the "establishment," which epitomized the ills and irrationality of the traditional distribution system. For a variety of reasons, however, highly pragmatic managers of mass merchandising firms found it advantageous to establish closer ties with large trading firms.

One such benefit is the ability of trading companies to supply the enormous volume of merchandise demanded by large retailing firms. This is particularly true in regard to products such as apparel and certain household items that traditionally have been manufactured and distributed by small firms, many of which have been closely tied to and controlled by large trading firms. The managements of mass merchandising firms found it advantageous to capitalize on the traditional leadership and expertise of trading companies in this field.

Another important line of products in which close ties with trading companies will undoubtedly prove beneficial to mass merchandising firms is fresh food: fish, meat, and vegetables. Fresh food traditionally has been marketed through the central wholesale markets, and this manner of distribution is not suitable to supermarket operations. To obtain fresh food in large volume, it is necessary to create new channels. To develop and manage such a system, the expertise of trading companies will be invaluable. Another potentially attractive feature is the extensive network of overseas procurement sources that large trading companies posess. The mass merchandising firms have begun to look toward foreign sources, particularly to Southeast Asia, for certain types of products in order to obtain cost advantages.

The second major advantage to large-scale retail firms of affiliation with trading companies is the access to huge financial resources that these large trading firms command. Trading companies not only are willing to extend liberal credit to rapidly growing mass merchandising firms, but are prepared to purchase store sites, build and equip new stores, and lease them to the chains.

For the trading companies, this alliance is extremely attractive, inasmuch as it gives them a foothold in this rapidly growing industry, in which they hitherto had had only limited participation. The alliance between these two forms typically goes far beyond commercial transactions. The potential ability of large trading companies to develop and supply original merchandise lines also benefits mass merchandising firms. For example, in early 1969 Seiyu entered into a four-year agreement with Mitsubishi Shoji, the world-famous trading company, a prominent member of the Mitsubishi group. Among other things, this agreement stipulated that Mitsubishi would extend ¥20 billion credit to Seiyu for the purpose of capital investment, and in return Seiyu committed itself to make up to 20 percent of its total purchases from Mitsubishi by 1972. In early 1969 Daiei and a number of other large supermarket chains entered into similar agreements with large trading companies. Jasco also entered into a cooperative arrangement with Mitsubishi Trading Company. Their collaboration will span a wide range of activities, including the development of shopping centers.

The third major advantage is the organization and management capability of major trading companies. We have noted earlier that one of the major problems facing large mass merchandising chains is the relative lack of managerial talent. Large trading companies, on the other hand, have abundant managerial resources. The ability of trading companies to mobilize and organize resources is particularly important, if not essential, to diversification efforts by mass merchandising firms. Especially advantageous is the fact that, not infrequently, large trading companies can mobilize resources from other firms belonging to the same group.

Indeed, this cooperation with trading companies has marked the beginning of a new era in the development of Japan's mass merchandising firms. It is now relevant to speculate about the possible impact of this development on mass merchandising firms. For example, one pertinent question that deserves careful scrutiny is the degree to which they can continue to pursue an independent course. Given their characteristic pragmatism, mass merchandising firms view their alliance with trading companies simply as a marriage of convenience and merely as the means to achieve their highly ambitious growth objectives. Managers of large mass merchandising firms are indeed aware of the potential pitfalls, and most have been careful in structuring their relationships with trading companies, particularly by seeking ties with several different trading companies. Nevertheless, given the enormous power that the trading companies command, and their increasingly aggressive posture toward the mass merchandising field, the emerging relationship deserves continuous scrutiny.

In this chapter we have examined the development of large-scale mass merchandising retail firms in postwar Japan. Without doubt, this development has had far-reaching impact and has been a key revolutionary force in the dynamically changing Japanese distribution sector.

CHAPTER

4

OTHER RECENT MARKETING DEVELOPMENTS

In this chapter we shall explore some of the other significant marketing developments in recent years which are of vital importance to American corporate managers interested in Japan. Included are marketing innovations by large manufacturers of consumer goods, the growth of self-service, the role of department stores, development of shopping centers, and growth of consumer credit.

MARKETING INNOVATIONS BY LARGE MANUFACTURERS OF CONSUMER GOODS

One of the most important developments in the postwar business scene is the great interest manifested in marketing by large manufacturers of consumer products. In this section, we shall examine the emergence of large marketing-oriented Japanese manufacturers. Of particular interest are the innovative approaches that have emerged in their distribution policy. In this section we shall identify major considerations which have forced manufacturers of Japanese consumer goods to take greater interest in marketing. We shall then examine some of the patterns of response that have evolved in certain key industries. Such an understanding is essential for American enterprises planning to do business in Japan.

Forces for Change

Until the end of World War II, large manufacturing firms, most of which belonged to a handful of Zaibatsu, confined their activities largely to heavy strategic arms industries. Consumer industries were virtually unknown; whatever ones that existed were rudimentary and confined in most cases, to small-scale cottage production. The output of these industries was sold through a myriad of small wholesalers and retailers; in linking these small manufacturers and marketing intermediaries, trading companies often played a critical role.

The situation in which large manufacturing firms found themselves in the aftermath of World War II was radically different. The Zaibatsu were dissolved by order of the Allied Occupation. The total disappearance of the military market meant that these large manufacturers now had to shift completely to peacetime industries. Amid these hardships Japan's consumer industries emerged.

Out of a rather humble beginning, the Japanese consumer industries were to blossom into a operation by any standard within a very short period of time. Japan now has the second-largest market for consumer products—second only to the United States. This is true in cosmetics, home appliances, automobiles, pharmaceuticals, synthetic fibers, and other industries.

As the consumer industries began to emerge, Japanese manufacturers became increasingly aware of the need to become involved in marketing activities for a variety of reasons: (1) the drive to expand capacity and obtain a greater share of the growing market; (2) the need for accurate information about the market, particularly about consumer tastes and trends (timely and accurate market information is vital for planning capacity, introducing new products, and planning production); and (3) the inability and unwillingness of the traditional distribution sector to meet the changed conditions created by the rapid rise in output level and the swift introduction of new products.

In the prewar era, it was quite common for manufacturers to relegate the entire distribution task to distributors and dealers. The manufacturing firms considered their task completed when the merchandise was shipped out of their warehouses. Often they did not know or care how their products were distributed. However, as the consumer industry emerged and developed in the postwar era, the highly atomized and typically small-scale marketing intermediaries became wholly inadequate to the task of distributing the ever-increasing flow of merchandise.

A classic example of this is the home appliance industry where the traditional wholesalers and retailers were still very small. The output of this industry grew nearly twentyfold during the 1960s. Moreover, a number of new items were introduced, most with high unit prices, such as refrigerators and television sets. It would certainly have been impossible for the small traditional marketing intermediaries to market their products without the extensive assistance in distribution provided by large manufacturers.

Responses to Changing Conditions

To market their products, the Japanese consumer industries have employed a number of innovative adaptations in several major ways. First, leading consumer-goods manufacturers have streamlined their internal organizations to strengthen marketing activities. Staff marketing units were created to complement the line marketing functions. These staff marketing groups included market research, customer services, credit analysis, inventory management, and distribution. In highly diversified firms, the divisional concept has been introduced to sharpen the company's marketing effectiveness, and to achieve better and more effective coordination between production and marketing.

The second innovation is extensive investment by major manufacturers in advertising activities. The total advertising expenditure for 1972 reached roughly $2 billion, and the bulk of this sum was spent by a small number of extremely large companies (see Table 4.1).

One of the most significant developments in the postwar Japanese marketing scene is the rather extensive control attained by large manufacturers of selected consumer goods over their channels of distribution. We have noted earlier that in most consumer-goods industries, large wholesalers and trading companies occupied a pivotal position in the distribution system prior to World War II. Indeed, they were the captains of the channel and held uncontested power over both small manufacturers and retailers.

With the emergence of large-scale consumer industries, the situation has undergone a significant change. In a number of instances large manufacturers have all but taken over the distribution functions, usually by bringing independent wholesalers and retailers under their control. As a result, in a number of consumer industries, we have witnessed the rise of distribution systems dominated and controlled by manufacturers. This pattern is found in those large consumer industries dominated by oligopolistic firms and those that have experienced extraordinarily rapid growth, including the automobile, electric home appliance, pharmaceutical, and cosmetic industries.

Evolution of a New Distribution System

Several forces have led to the new distribution pattern. First, manufacturers have been making intense efforts to build strong national brands by appealing directly to consumers. To the extent that this is successful, it tends to weaken the power of marketing intermediaries.

TABLE 4.1

Advertising Expenditures
by Major Japanese Corporations, 1971

	¥ Million	Percentage of Increase Over Previous Year	Percentage of Sales
Matsushita Electric	14,873	112.1	2.01
Toshiba	11,283	120.5	1.92
Nissan	10,227	126.6	1.39
Takedo Pharmaceuticals	8,999	108.9	5.26
Toyota	8,694	119.8	1.00
Mitsubishi Electric	8,108	114.2	2.04
Hitachi	7,610	126.2	1.01
Sanyo Electric	6,949	119.0	2.87
Kao Soap	6,683	115.5	12.29
Shiseido	6,624	110.5	6.49
Honda	6,024	110.5	2.12

Source: Company records.

Another important reason lies in the inability of old-style marketing intermediaries to cope with the new demand placed on them by the emergence of a mass market and the appearance of new products. As we have seen, marketing intermediaries were small, highly fragmented, seriously undercapitalized, and had only limited space. They tried to perform the distribution function under the new conditions, but were incapable of handling the avalanche of products, and there were no other institutions to handle the situation.

By trial and error, the manufacturers evolved a distribution system. To keep the loyalty of wholesalers and retailers, each of the major manufacturers sought to diversify into full lines of consumer electronics and home appliances. Thus, the large companies began to compete against one another in almost every principal product line. The major companies also created separate subsidiaries in the early 1960s to handle installment credit sales. Thanks to the introduction of mass production techniques, production costs had declined sharply in the late 1950s, and this generated extra revenue for marketing investment. Manufacturers used these extra resources as incentives to wholesalers and retailers to encourage them to intensify their efforts. Generous rebates were given and the payment terms were quite liberal.

It is difficult to estimate accurately how much investment each of the major companies made in building its national sales network, but by noting their investment in the form of equity ownership in wholesalers and other distributors one can glimpse the intensity of their efforts. For example, in 1961 Toshiba had invested ¥1.2 billion in marketing intermediaries, Sanyo ¥70 million, and Matsushita ¥600 million. Six years later, these investments grew to ¥2.8 billion, ¥2.3 billion and ¥5.1 billion respectively. If investment in other forms, particularly credit extended, were to be included, the total financial commitment by the manufacturers in their marketing operations would have been considerably greater than indicated.

The Appliance and Electronics Industries

Appliance wholesalers were under great pressure from the manufacturers to pursue similar strategies in order to encourage their retailers to intensify their marketing efforts. The wholesalers followed with liberal rebates and credit to certain retailers. Since the demand for appliances were growing rapidly, for a few years the condition perpetuated itself without drastic results. By the early 1960s, however, major home appliances reached a turning point.

The rapid expansion of production capacity finally caught up with what had once appeared to be an insatiable demand. The industry began to experience cutthroat competition. Ever anxious to expand their market share, the manufacturers refused to make quick downward adjustments of their level of production. Instead, they intensified their promotional efforts, applying even greater pressures on marketing intermediaries. In many cases, they literally attempted to dump their products into these channels by offering almost every conceivable type of incentives, rebates, and discounts. Lured by these incentives, wholesalers and retailers took on added inventories. Manufacturers, in their attempt to broaden their coverage, competed vigorously and often indiscriminately to bring even the smallest and weakest retailer under their control.

The consequences of these ill-conceived and shortsighted sales approaches were obvious. Price cutting became commonplace; there were excess inventories at every stage of the channels. Coupled with frequent model changes, such heavy stocks encouraged price cutting. Consumers then refused to pay list prices. Many retailers and wholesalers were on the verge of bankruptcy. By the end of the 1960s the situation deteriorated to a point where manufacturers were compelled to take some action.

Recognizing the danger of these developments, the major manufacturers began to streamline their distribution structure. First, these companies sought to establish an exclusive sales territory for each sales subsidiary or wholesaler. One of the major reasons for the fierce price competition was that a number of wholesalers associated with a given manufacturer competed vigorously to woo retailers within the same territory. In order to obviate this situation, a manufacturer selected one firm in a given territory and sought to strengthen its ties. This effort usually succeeded. It is commonly observed now that most wholesalers are affiliated with one of the several manufacturers and the latter owns at least 50 percent equity in these distributors. Thus, wholesalers are in effect owned and controlled by the manufacturers.

The second step was the creation of specialized installment sales subsidiaries. Up until this time, the installment sales companies created by the manufacturers throughout the nation had been engaged in actual marketing tasks themselves. This created some confusion, and gave rise to the possibility that retailers could play a regular wholesaler against an installment sales company. To avoid these problems, the installment sales company was made into a financing company whose sole function was to provide support to retail stores.

Still a third step was for manufacturers to become more discriminating in the selection of retail outlets, and to clarify their relationship with them. To strengthen their ties with retail outlets on a selective basis, manufacturers sought to classify them into several categories according to the degree of their willingness to be associated. For example, Toshiba classified its retail outlets into four groups, according to size. There were some 4,000 outlets which derived 80 percent of their total sales from Toshiba products. Matsushita has an association of some 20,000 retail outlets which derive at least 50 percent of their total sales from Matsushita products. Of these there are about 7,000 stores which obtain over 80 percent of their total sales from Matsushita products. And, converseley, in the case of Matsushita, these stores alone are responsible for 80 percent of total Matsushita sales.

Thus, there is a gradual trend toward greater concentration of a manufacturer's sales in a relatively small percentage of Japan's retail stores. This is particularly notable among "big ticket" items. For example, among the Matsushita-affiliated retailers, it is estimated that 10 percent of the retail outlets sell 90 percent of such major items as color television sets, refrigerators, and air conditioners. Consumers tend to purchase less expensive items in neighborhood stores. It is estimated that 75 percent of these small items are purchased within a half-mile radius of the customer's home.

Against this background, in the mid-1960s a number of significant new developments began to appear. The first were the rapid gains recorded by mass merchandising firms. In 1968, Daiei, the largest mass merchandising firm in the country, sold roughly ¥10 billion worth of home appliances, accounting for 13 percent of its total sales. The following year sales increased to ¥15 billion, and by 1970, they were up to ¥20 billion. More significantly, Daiei began to market some of its standard products under its own brand name. Then the company took over the control of a medium size manufacturer of key consumer electronic products (notably radios and television sets) and created a sensation by selling 17-inch color sets for less than ¥60,000, against the then prevailing price of ¥90,000.

The second significant trend was the development of independent chain outlets not associated with a particular manufacturer. Two major independent chains have become of significant size. One of these is now responsible for 14 percent of the total national sale of home appliances. These developments are threatening the dominance that manufacturers had gained over the distribution channels. Thus, the situation is indeed very fluid.

The Cosmetic Industry

One of the most effective and smoothly functioning distribution systems has been developed by the leading Japanese firms in the cosmetic industry. This industry has been growing very rapidly in Japan during the past two decades. By 1971, it had developed into a ¥180 billion industry, second only to that of the United States. There are about 150 cosmetics manufacturers of various sizes, but over half the sales are made by the five leading manufacturers. Among the five, the most successful is Shiseido, which has painstakingly built up one of the most effective distribution systems in Japan. Shiseido enjoys more than a third of the domestic cosmetic market. The company derives roughly 80 percent of its sales from cosmetics and the remaining 20 percent from other kinds of toiletries.

To distribute its cosmetic products, the company divided the entire nation into 73 territories. In each territory it established a wholesaling subsidiary in which Shiseido own the controlling, if not the majority, interest. These sales subsidiaries, in turn, sell to some 13,000 controlled or affiliated retail outlets, including virtually all of Japan's outstanding cosmetic retail concerns. They are independent stores, but they are known as Shiseido Chain Stores.

Many of the large retail outlets generally set aside a certain portion of store space for Shiseido products, known as the "Shiseido Corner," and the company provides attractive display cases as well as point-of-sale promotional devices. These chain outlets are organized into six categories according to their sales volume, and the company has a separate discount policy for each category. As one of the conditions for chain membership, retail firms are required to agree to resale price maintenance at the retail level. The company has several thousand beauty consultants who visit these retail outlets at regular intervals to perform demonstration services for customers.

The company distributes its toiletries through the Shiseido Trading Company, a wholly owned subsidiary, which in turn sells to some 400 wholesalers, which sell to 100,000 retail outlets. In both cosmetics and toiletries the company controls the price structure of its products at every stage of distribution. Shiseido maintains its control over the distribution channels through the effective combination of ownership, administrative relationship, and contractual ties. The company places a great deal of emphasis on trade relations and has a large complement of staff personnel assigned to this function.

The company's outstanding success owes much to its imaginative distribution policy. This policy has enabled the company to establish an orderly distribution pattern, to avoid price-cutting in a highly competitive industry, in which such a practice is extremely common, and to encourage active sales efforts by retailers. As we noted earlier, the company's organizational efforts have gone even beyond retail outlets by establishing a direct link with customer clubs. Thus the company has skillfully organized its entire marketing channel up to and including the ultimate consumer.

The Pharmaceutical Industry

Pharmaceuticals provide another example of the attempt by large manufacturers to develop a vertically integrated distribution system. The Japanese pharmaceutical industry has also achieved very rapid growth in the postwar period. During the decade ending in 1968 the value of output of this industry grew fivefold, reaching the ¥700 billion level. The Japanese pharmaceutical industry is second only to that of the United States in world sales. Unlike the home appliance industry, it is made up of some 2,000 to 3,000 manufacturers of various sizes and descriptions. These manufacturers range from small shops with no more than three or four employees to a firm with more than 10,000 employees whose annual sales exceed ¥127 billion. A dozen or so leading manufacturers are responsible for over 50 percent of the total pharmaceutical sales. Another characteristic of this industry is its sheer number of products. According to one estimate there are some 20,000 different items currently available on the market, and new products are constantly being introduced.

This industry, too, traditionally had been dominated by large wholesalers; in fact, some of the prominent manufacturers began as wholesalers. The distribution channel has been circuitous and complicated, with a myriad of primary and secondary wholesalers and small retail outlets. According to the latest Commercial Census, there are some 39,000 retail outlets and 3,500 wholesalers handling pharmaceutical products.

The pharmaceutical industry responded to the rapidly growing demand in a manner typical of other growth industries in postwar Japan. Large manufacturers, having reequiped themselves with the most up-to-date production facilities, increased their capacity rapidly and introduced a large number of new products by taking advantage of licensed foreign technology. Medium-sized and small manufacturing establishments tried hard to keep up with their larger competitors. Characteristically, they competed vigorously to seek a greater share of the growing market. Here again a familiar situation of oversupply and extensive price cutting developed. In fact, by the early 1960s the pharmaceutical industry had become one of the most competitive industries in Japan, characterized by frequent discounting practices.

To combat this situation, major manufacturers began to seek greater control over certain wholesale, and particularly retail, outlets. The aforementioned characteristics of the industry make it difficult to achieve this objective. Because of the large number of products, obviously no single manufacturer, regardless of size, can possibly supply the entire range of products to wholesale and retail outlets. As a result, in seeking to establish a network of affiliated outlets, large manufacturers in this industry are in a weaker position than those in less diversified industries, such as home appliances. Aware of their limited power, they tend to emphasize cooperation rather than control in forging a network of affiliated outlets. In fact, it is not uncommon for a retail firm to belong to several different manufacturers' groups. To offset this disadvantage, however, pharmaceutical manufacturers do enjoy one important advantage not commonly shared by other manufacturers: pharmaceuticals are one of the few industries in which resale price maintenance is permitted legally. In attempting to develop a network of affiliated outlets, large pharmaceutical manufacturers have made good use of this legal provision.

Let us examine patterns developed by several leading firms. Tanabe Seiyaku was the first among the major firms to attempt to organize marketing intermediaries. This network includes about 100 wholesalers and nearly 13,000 retail drug outlets, covering some 60 items. The company divided the country into 172 market areas, and affiliated wholesalers and retailers in each area were organized into an association that, in turn, is a member of the nationwide federation. The officers of this federation consist primarily of representatives of retail outlets, supplemented by persons representing the wholesalers and the manufacturing companies. The representatives of this federation are consulted regularly on important matters affecting them, such as new product introduction and credit terms. Tanabe gives special promotional and managerial assistance to these stores. Other major pharmaceutical manufacturers have followed suit. Takeda Seiyaku, the largest pharmaceutical manufacturer, though the last one to adopt this approach, is estimated to have more than 23,000 affiliated retail outlets.

In discussion of both pharmaceutical and cosmetic industries, references have been made to resale price maintenance by manufacturers. The resale price maintenance agreement is, indeed, a potent weapon for large manufacturers, allowing them to legally bind actions of their wholesale and retail outlets. Because of extensive reliance made on this practice by manufactureres in some industries, we shall discuss it in greater detail.

Price Maintenance

Price maintenance is legally prohibited under Japan's Antimonopoly Act, which was enacted immediately after World War II; but certain products are exempted from this Act. Initially, nine product categories were exempted, but four subsequently have been taken off the list. In 1969, resale price maintenance was legally allowed for the following product groups: cosmetics, dyes, toothpaste, soap for home use, and drugs. There are some 4,000 specific items within these broad categories.

As indicated in Table 4.2, the number of manufacturing firms that engage in resale price maintenance has been increasing steadily during the past 13 years. Growing competitive pressure and a rising trend toward price-cutting in those industries in which the practice is allowed are considered to be the major reasons for this increase. While the total annual sales of the products covered by resale price maintenance agreements are estimated to account for only about 2 percent of total retail sales, in some industries they are extremely important. For example, in cosmetics sales virtually all the major firms insist on resale price maintenance for certain products. It is estimated that the products covered by this practice account for as high as 85 percent of total cosmetic sales. It is further estimated that altogether as many as 42,000 wholesalers and retailers are bound by resale price agreements of some sort. In those industries in which this practice is allowed, it is a very potent weapon for

TABLE 4.2

Number of Japanese Manufacturers Requiring Resale
Price Maintenance for Selected Products, 1962-68

Year	Cosmetics	Toothpaste	Soap	Drugs
1962	30	2	4	1
1963	30	2	4	5
1964	33	2	4	14
1965	34	4	6	29
1966	35	4	7	36
1967	34	2	9	39
1968	34	2	9	44

Source: "White Paper on National Life" (Tokyo: The Economic Planning Agency, 1969), pp. 282-283.

manufacturers to use in establishing and maintaining control over the channels of distribution.

In addition, even in those industries in which resale price maintenance is not permitted legally, large manufacturers are engaged in covert or underground attempts to control prices and terms of sale at various levels of the channel. For several reasons, the Japanese government was lax, at least until recently, in enforcing the Antimonopoly Act, including preventing companies from resorting to informal agreements to control the price structure through various channels.

By the sheer power that these large manufacturing firms enjoy vis-à-vis their distributors, they can bind to an important degree the actions of their marketing intermediaries. They are often in a position to exert strong pressure against recalcitrants, including refusal to sell to distributors who are not responsive to manufacturers' requirements. A recent estimate by the Fair Trade Commission indicates that these "underground" or "informal" arrangements for resale price maintenance affect transactions totaling some ¥2,300 billion, accounting for some 20 percent of total retail sales.

Conclusion

We have seen how large manufacturers in certain industries have taken over leadership in the distribution system. In many cases, these patterns have been developed not by conscious design or strategy but through a series of groping experiments as a by-product of the search for better alternatives to traditional methods, especially after the mass production of consumer goods made the old channels ineffective.

It is significant to note, however, that within a very short time in a number of industries we have witnessed the emergence of a well-organized and disciplined manufacturer-controlled distribution system. In doing so, manufacturers have devised a variety of ingenious means and by and large have been flexible and pragmatic. The patterns thus emerging range from tightly controlled and autocratic relationships, as in the case of automobiles or even home appliances, to the cooperative and democratic type, as in the case of the pharmaceutical industry. The degree of success, of course, depends on a number of factors, but to an important measure, it is related to large manufacturers' ability:

1. To establish a strong consumer franchise for their products through aggressive promotion.
2. To extend financial and managerial assistance to selected marketing intermediaries.
3. To develop alternate channels, if necessary.
4. To bind marketing intermediaries legally on resale price and terms of sale, or to insist on informal "understandings" on resale price maintenance.

The apparent success achieved in a number of industries is largely due, of course, to intense efforts by manufacturers, but it is interesting to speculate on the degree to which such efforts have been facilitated by a strongly entrenched collectivity orientation, particularly of the hierarchical type, in Japanese cultural tradition. At least, manufacturers' appeals for group solidarity and identification, when appropriately supported by practical incentives, are consistent with a dominant aspect of Japanese cultural heritage.

GROWTH OF SELF-SERVICE

We have noted earlier that the self-service concept is now employed extensively by large-scale mass merchandising chains; but it is not confined to large-scale retailers alone. It is also employed by single unit, small retail establishments and some large-scale wholesale firms. Although the concept of self-service is closely related to the development of large-scale mass merchandising firms, because of its significance we shall give it separate treatment here.

The self-service concept is strictly a postwar phenomenon, having been first introduced in Tokyo in 1953. Its applicability to Japan

TABLE 4.3

Growth of the Self-Service Concept in Japan,
1964-70

Date	Number of Stores	Number of Employees	Annual Sales (¥100 million)
1964	3,620	87,000	3,924
1966	4,790	105,000	5,811
1968	7,062	143,000	10,286
1970	9,403	173,000	16,125
		Percent Change	
1964-66	32.2	20.7	48.1
1966-68	47.6	36.2	77.0
1968-70	33.1	21.0	56.8
1964-70	159.8	98.9	310.9

Source: Ministry of International Trade and Industry, 1971.

was almost universally questioned, because at that time it represented the complete antithesis to traditional retailing practices commonly accepted in Japan. Elaborate service was one of the important sales devices employed by prestigious stores before the spread of mass merchandising. Certainly, few businessmen predicted the very rapid rate at which this rather radical innovation would be accepted by the average Japanese consumer. Indeed, it has now become widely diffused, and consumers have come to expect self-service as the modus operandi of supermarkets.

Self-service stores are not primarily confined to urban centers, but are well diffused throughout the nation. Only slightly more than 10 percent of all self-service stores are found in the seven metropolitan centers.

The rapid growth of self-service stores can be seen partially from the statistics presented in Table 4.3*. From their modest beginning in Tokyo in 1953, these stores in aggregate accounted for

---

*Some numbers for self-service stores in this section vary from those given in Tables 34 to 37, due to different definition of categories.

about 8 percent of total retail sales in 1970. Between 1968 and 1970 the number of establishments using self-service increased more than 33 percent, the number of employees increased 21 percent and sales made in such stores increased almost 57 percent. When we look at the longer period, 1964 to 1970, we see the same trends exaggerated: the number of stores increased nearly 160 percent, while the number of employees increased less than 100 percent, but the amount of sales increased more than 310 percent. Although these figures suggest strikingly that personnel is being used more sparingly and more effectively, we must at the same time remember that the sales figure reflects price inflation as well as increased volume of merchandise.

There is additional evidence, however, that there has been a steady trend toward increased efficiency among self-service stores. The data will be presented in Table 4.5 following a discussion of the increasing size of the individual stores.

Having examined the rapid growth of the self-service concept in Japan, we shall now examine the operating characteristics of these stores. A typical self-service store is much smaller than its American counterpart, although it is considerably larger than a regular retail store in Japan. According to the Commercial Census of 1970, a typical self-service store had annual sales of ¥171 million or $570,000, employed 19 full-time employees, and had approximately 4,700 square feet of sales space. Looking at the distribution of self-service stores by size (Table 4.4), we find that in 1970 (the latest year for which statistics are available) over 58 percent of the self-service stores in Japan consisted of establishments with sales floor space of less than 300 square meters (3240 square feet). More than 90 percent of these establishments had less than 1,000 square meters (10,800 square feet) of sales space. The trend to note, however, is that even in a brief two-year period, the percentage of stores above 600 square meters of sales space is shown to be consistently increasing.

Similarly, when we look at sales, the volume is small, but it is growing. As is evident in Table 4.5 over 59 percent of the stores had annual sales of less than ¥100 million ($330,000) in 1970. Roughly 23 percent had an annual sales volume of less than ¥300 million (approximately $1 million) that year. However, as the percentage change in sales between 1966 and 1970 shown on Table 4.5 makes clear, the share of sales made by larger stores is increasing impressively, while that of the smaller stores is decreasing. Again, the relationship to note is that while the sales proportion of the larger stores is increasing, the number of employees per 100 square meters of sales space is decreasing for these stores. The selling is being accomplished with fewer employees, and this is highly important in a country with a labor shortage, as is the case in Japan.

TABLE 4.4

Distribution of Self-Service Stores by
Size of Sales Space, 1968-70

Sales Space (in square meters)*	Number of Stores 1968	Number of Stores 1970	Percent of Total 1968	Percent of Total 1970
100-199	3027	3862	42.9	41.1
200-299	1198	1635	17.0	17.4
300-399	966	1141	13.4	12.1
400-599	735	1016	10.4	10.8
600-999	589	868	8.3	9.2
1,000-1,499	333	474	4.7	5.0
1,500 & over	214	407	3.0	4.3
Total	7062	9403	100.0	100.0

*One square meter equals 10.8 square feet.

Source: Commercial Census, 1970.

Table 4.6 presents several pertinent indexes of performance for self-service stores according to the size of store in terms of sales space. Sales per store increase steeply with the size of store. Sales per employee also increase directly with the size of store, but not nearly so dramatically. Operating expenses as a percentage of sales remain almost constant regardless of the size of store. Wages as a percent of sales varies inversely with the size of store.

When classified by merchandise category, nearly 58 percent of sales by self-service stores come from food and related items, 23 percent from apparel and the rest are scattered among miscellaneous merchandise and restaurants. Interestingly, wholesale transactions account for slightly over 3 percent of the total self-service sales.

THE ROLE OF DEPARTMENT STORES

Japan's department stores have gone through dynamic changes in the last decade. Until the early 1960s department stores had dominated the Japanese retail scene. According to Japan's Department

Store Law, a department store is defined as a store with departmentalized lines of merchandise, and in the seven urban centers having at least 3,000 square meters (roughly 32,400 square feet) of sales space; outside these cities, the minimum sales space is 1,500 square meters. This type of store accounts for slightly over 10 percent of total retail sales in Japan.

A typical department store in 1970 was something like the following: it had annual sales of approximately ¥7 billion, with sales space of about 150,000 square feet, and employed 570 people. Since the average retail store in Japan had an annual sales volume of less than ¥7 million and only three employees, the contrast is indeed marked. While the foregoing facts present a composite picture of an average department store, there are significant differences in size within the department store category. It ranges from an extremely large firm such as Mitsukoshi, with eleven stores under its direct control, whose annual sales exceed ¥180 billion, to relatively small stores whose annual sales are no larger than ¥2 billion.

TABLE 4.5

Distribution of Employees and Sales
in Self-Service Stores by Size of Store, 1966-70

Sales Space (square meters)*	Number of Employees per 100 Square Meters 1968	1970	Percentage of Sales Volume 1966	1968	1970	Percentage of Change in Sales 1968-70	1966-70
100-199	8.5	5.7	19.5	15.8	13.5	-2.3	-6.0
200-299	7.1	4.9	12.2	10.5	9.3	-1.2	-2.9
300-399	7.5	4.7	12.2	11.0	9.5	-1.5	-2.7
400-599	6.1	4.2	14.1	12.8	11.8	-1.0	-2.3
600-999	5.1	3.8	16.4	15.3	15.3	0	-1.1
1000-1499	5.7	4.0	10.2	16.4	17.3	+0.9	+7.1
1500 & over	5.0	3.1	15.3	18.2	23.3	+5.9	+8.0
Total	6.7	4.1	100	100	100	—	—

*One square meter equals 10.8 square feet.

Source: Commercial Census, 1970.

TABLE 4.6

Performance Data of Self-Service Stores by Size of Store, 1970

Sales Space (square meters)*	Average Sales per Store (¥10,000)	Average Sales per Employee (¥10,000)	Operating Expenses (percentage of sales)	Wages (percentage of sales)	Stock Turnover
100-199	5,645	6,969	12.9	6.3	12.7
200-299	9,164	7,608	13.4	6.3	13.3
300-399	13,391	8,296	13.4	6.1	14.3
400-599	18,737	9,030	13.2	5.8	14.9
600-999	28,425	9,957	12.8	5.2	14.5
1000-1499	58,810	11,867	12.4	4.5	14.3
1500 & Over	92,427	10,952	13.1	4.7	11.7

*One square meter equals 10.8 square feet.

Source: Commercial Census, 1970.

Basically Japanese department stores can be classified into three major types. The first type has grown out of traditional dry goods stores and are the country's original and most prestigious stores. The origins of a number of these stores go back as early as the 16th century. Among them, the largest and most prestigious are Matsuzakaya, Mitsukoshi, Daimaru, and Takashimaya. These stores are located in the major metropolitan areas, notably Tokyo.

The second type of stores are those owned and managed by private railroad lines in metropolitan areas, primarily in Tokyo, Osaka, and Nagoya. As part of their diversification strategy, some of the major railroads built department stores at their main terminals. With the rapid growth of suburban communities, these stores have been extremely successful. Examples of these stores are Odakyu, Seibu, and Keio.

The third type are those known as local department stores. They are located in large regional cities outside of the major urban centers and are considerably smaller than a typical store falling into either of the previous two types. They are likely to have grown out of small independent retail stores.

Only 22 percent of the department stores are located in the six major cities, and the rest are scattered throughout Japan. These big-city stores comprise roughly two-thirds of the total sales by all department stores. They account for about half the total floor space of all department stores in Japan. The sales of department stores outside the major metropolitan areas, however, are increasing at a much faster pace than are those in the six largest cities. Note the differences in rate of increase between 1960 and 1968 shown in Table 4.7.

During the past decade and a half, the number of department stores nationally almost doubled and their total retail sales grew twenty times, yet their share of total retail sales remained unchanged because retail sales have grown at roughly the same rate as department stores during this period. The recent increase of sales by department stores is presented in Table 4.8. The national rate of year-to-year increase doubled between 1965 and 1970, from 10.1 percent from 1964-65 to 20.4 percent in 1969-70. Riding on the crest of the rapid expansion of the consumer market, the department stores have achieved a substantial growth during the past several years, as evidenced by both Tables 4.7 and 4.8.*

---

*Some data for department stores in this section vary from those given in Tables 34 to 37 due to different definition of categories —particularly the separate treatment of installment department stores in Tables 34 to 37.

TABLE 4.7

Total Sales of Department Stores, 1960-68
(1965=100)

Year	Total Sales	Department Store in Six Metropolitan Areas	Department Store Outside of the Major Metropolitan Areas
1960	47.3	51.0	39.6
1961	58.5	63.3	48.3
1962	68.3	73.6	57.0
1963	79.8	84.9	69.1
1964	90.8	93.6	84.9
1965	100.0	100.0	100.0
1966	112.2	110.4	116.1
1967	128.9	124.6	138.0
1968	150.4	142.2	167.6

Source: "Monthly Report on Department Store Sales, December 1968" (Tokyo: The Ministry of International Trade and Industry, 1969), p. 4.

Merchandise carried by Japanese department stores is quite similar to that of their American counterparts. The average department store sales are 43 percent soft goods, 15 percent household furnishings including home appliances, 13 percent furniture, 7 percent sundry goods, and 22 percent miscellaneous services. A significant characteristic of the Japanese department store is the wide range of services it offers its customers. Its past success is partly credited to the great emphasis it has placed on creating a prestige-oriented, luxurious, shopping atmosphere and meticulous personal service. A typical large department store in an urban center has theaters, restaurants, child care centers, and other customer service facilities. It also sponsors exhibits, concerts, and lecture series as well as lessons in a variety of subjects.

While the department stores sales have increased at a rapid rate during the past decade, their once uncontested leadership as the only large-scale retail establishment in Japan has been seriously challenged by the new mass merchandising firms, as described in Chapter 3. In the mid-1960s the relative position of department stores deteriorated considerably. The department stores hit their lowest ebb in 1966 and since have been waging aggressive and often

TABLE 4.8

Growth of Department Store Sales, 1965-70

	National Total ¥ billion	Percent Increase	Stores Located in Urban Centers ¥ billion	Percent Increase	Stores Located Outside 7 Major Cities ¥ billion	Percent Increase
1965	929.4	10.1	629.9	6.8	299.5	17.8
1966	1,042.7	12.2	695.0	10.3	347.8	16.1
1967	1,198.1	14.9	784.7	12.9	413.4	18.9
1968	1,397.8	16.7	895.9	14.4	501.9	21.4
1969	1,650.5	18.1	1,053.6	17.6	597.0	18.9
1970	1,986.6	20.4	1,252.9	18.9	733.7	22.9

Source: The Commercial Census, 1971, p. 68.

TABLE 4.9

Financial and Operating Results
of Selected Department Stores, 1968

Gross margin as percent of sales	21.6
Selling and administrative expenses as percent of sales	18.1
Net operating income as percent of sales	3.5
Net other income as percent of sales	0.7
Net profit before tax (percent)	2.7
Net income after tax (percent)	1.6
Annual stock turnover (times)	22.6
Annual capital turnover (times)	2.4
Before-tax return on total capital (percent)	6.9
Return on equity (percent)	24.4
Equity as percent of total capital	28.1

Source: Department Store Statistics, 1968 (Tokyo: The Japan Department Store Association, 1969), p. 44.

successful campaigns to regain their leadership position. The day is indeed gone when they can command an unchallenged leadership position in retailing. Although Mitsukoshi is still the largest retail firm in terms of total sales, the second place is occupied by Daiei, a supermarket chain, and it is predicted that the latter will soon overtake the former.

Table 4.9 presents the overall picture of financial and operating results of Japanese department stores. However, gross margins and stock turnover vary among major categories of merchandise. Note the following statistics:

	Clothing	Housewares	Foods	Total
Gross margins	26.0	20.1	18.0	22.6
Stock turnover	13.6	20.7	19.9	18.8

Also, to gain an overview of the structure of department stores in Japan, it is essential to distinguish between the characteristics found among firms of different sizes. There exist major differences in operating efficiency according to the size of the stores. Economy of scale is clearly evident in the operations of department stores

TABLE 4.10

Financial and Performance Characteristics of Department Stores
in Japanese Cities of Various Sizes, 1970

	A	B	C	D	E	F	G
Sales per firm (¥100 million)	657	187	67	32	30	15	12
Average number of stores per firm	3.5	2.9	1.5	1.3	1.3	1.0	1.0
Size of store (in tsubos)*	7,154	4,381	3,430	2,208	2,208	1,602	1,495
Sales per tsubo	2,623	1,474	1,308	1,104	1,108	950	824
Sales per employee (¥1,000)	15,767	9,558	9,603	8,123	7,412	6,509	5,757
Cost of goods sold	77.6	76.0	78.2	79.3	73.2	78.8	79.0
Gross margin	22.4	22.0	21.8	20.7	21.8	21.2	21.0
Wages and salaries	7.7	8.3	8.8	8.6	9.0	9.7	9.5
Other expenses	14.7	13.7	13.0	12.1	12.8	11.5	11.5
Profit before taxes	3.4	3.4	2.1	1.4	1.1	1.2	1.0

A. Stores located in cities over 2 million population and with annual sales of ¥50 billion or more.
B. Stores located in cities with a population of from 1 to 2 million, with sales between ¥20 billion to ¥50 billion.
C. Stores located in cities with a population of 500,000 to 1 million, with annual sales between ¥5 to 10 billion.
D. Stores located in cities with a population of 300,000 to 500,000, with annual sales of ¥2 to 5 billion.
E. Stores located in cities with a population of 300,000 to 500,000, with annual sales of less than ¥2 billion.
F. Stores located in cities with a population of less than 300,000, with annual sales of more than ¥2 billion.
G. Stores located in cities with a population of less than 300,000, with annual sales of less than ¥2 billion.

*One tsubo equals roughly 3.954 square yards.

Source: Miyakawa et al, Shin Ryutsu Saogyo, p. 100.

TABLE 4.11

Monthly Sales per Employee
According to Number of Employees, 1970
(in billions of yen)

Number of Employees	Total Sales per Employee
50- 99	633
100- 299	721
300- 499	771
500- 999	984
1,000-1,999	1,315
2,000 or more	1,536

Source: Commercial Census, 1971.

TABLE 4.12

Monthly Sales per Employee
According to Size of Store, 1970

Size of Store (square meters* of sales space)	Total Sales per Employee
1,500- 2,999	34
3,000- 4,999	35
5,000- 9,999	31
10,000-19,999	39
20,000-29,999	54
30,000 or more	78

*One square meter equals 10.8 square feet.

Source: Commercial Census, 1971.

(see Table 4.10). Differences among department stores by size are also significant in the data in Tables 4.11 and 4.12.

There are significant differences in profits before taxes among different size categories. This item, as well as "other expenses," gets smaller as the size of store diminishes. Moreover, the smaller the firm, the higher the ratio of wages as a percentage of total expenses.

For a variety of reasons, department stores face a serious challenge from emerging mass merchandising firms, as mentioned earlier. Let us briefly examine the major threats of which alert businessmen should be aware.

Threats to Traditional Department Stores

Perhaps the most serious problem is the failure of the management of some traditional department stores to grasp the implications of changes in consumption trends, particularly the emergence of the mass market and geographic shifts in the population. Department stores have always catered to the high-income class and older customers. Some managers have failed to broaden their appeal to encompass the rapidly rising new middle class. The prestigious department stores attract a large number of potential shoppers from the rising middle class, but these people simply enjoy the atmosphere, examine the merchandise, and then go to mass merchandising outlets where they can obtain similar items at lower prices.

The rapid growth of the suburbs has also contributed to the decline of department stores, particularly those located in downtown areas of the major cities. Until recently, department stores had not sought out these customers as aggressively as had major supermarket chains and discount stores.

Another challenge to department stores is the growth and penetration of national brands, now aggressively promoted by large manufacturers of consumer products. This has made the prestige and reputation of the place of purchase much less important. There is no doubt that the very sudden appearance of mass merchandising firms has posed a serious threat to the competitive viability of department stores.

Another challenge facing the department store is the rapid rise of the wage level. Given the high personal service content of their operations, this has seriously eroded the profitability of department stores, particularly smaller ones.

It is difficult to deny that until recently the managers of department stores had been complacent. They had been the dominant retail establishments in the country and their managers did not comprehend the changes that threatened them. The management of department stores cannot however, be held totally responsible for their failure to keep up with mass merchandise firms; they have been operating under serious handicaps. They have been severely constrained by the Department Store Law (and other regulations) the purpose of which is to protect small retailers against the threat of the large department stores. This Law places a number of restrictions on department stores, such as the requirement of government approval to open a department store, to add new branches, or even to expand the existing stores. The Law also regulates the number of days a week that department stores can be open as well as the store hours. Particularly serious to the department stores is the requirement that they obtain the government's approval for expansion of the existing stores, as well as for opening new ones. Each application must be screened by the Council on Department Stores, the advisory body to the Ministry of International Trade and Industry. Also particularly detrimental to the department store has been the fact that through legal loopholes, rather similar mass merchandising firms have been virtually unaffected by the Department Store Law.

Response to the Challenge

While these factors present challenges to the traditional department stores, in the past several years they have been making serious strides toward counteracting the threats. Large stores have been notably successful in their efforts. Let us consider various strategies that are now being pursued by them:

First, they have improved, and sometimes expanded, their downtown stores to attract customers back to the urban centers. The metropolitan areas are also combating deterioration by steadily improving their facilities, particularly public transportation. Second, major department stores have been aggressively seeking opportunities to open new stores in the rapidly growing suburban areas. Third, a number of progressive stores have been pursuing active diversification programs, including entering into supermarkets, real estate development, shopping centers and related activities. Fourth, the leading metropolitan department stores are now actively seeking opportunities to extend their assets through acquisition of smaller department stores by purchase, equity participation, or other means. Thus, although most of the local department stores maintain the outward semblance of independence, a number of them have become affiliated with major stores. A hieriarchal network is emerging with a large metropolitan department store at its peak, and a number of smaller regional department stores loosely affiliated with the major store. Finally, department stores are improving and streamlining their internal management practices. They are introducing new concepts such as chain operations, improving their inventory control system, and installing labor saving methods.

Thus, a number of leading department stores, having recognized the rapidly changing environment, are now attempting to adopt new strategies. In these attempts, they have several advantages that they can capitalize on. First, they have substantially more financial resources than have newly emerging large-scale retail establishments. They enjoy long-established banking connections. Moreover, many of the leading department stores have considerable real estate carried on their books at very nominal figures. This real estate can be disposed of to finance their expansion, or can be used as the locations for new stores.

Second, some department stores, notably those owned and managed by railroad interests, derive a significant competitive advantage from being part of a well diversified business. Most of them have a wide range of interests—real estate development, housing, sightseeing, and leisure related activities.

Third, large department stores have excellent managerial resources. True, top management of many of the leading department stores has been rather conservative in its outlook, but they do have a potentially excellent cadre of managerial personnel. Until recently, they had been the only retail institution that regularly recruited college graduates and attempted to give them extensive training. Finally, although this is an intangible advantage, department stores have a long-standing carry-over of the high prestige and reputation that they have traditionally enjoyed.

DEVELOPMENT OF SHOPPING CENTERS

Among major innovations in the Japanese marketing system is the emergence of shopping centers. For some time, Japan has had a semblance of shopping centers in which a number of specialty shops were housed under one roof. They have generally taken the form of shopping arcades and are concentrated in downtown areas of large cities and major railroad terminals in urban centers. These traditional clusters of shops are, however, different from an American-style shopping center in their basic concepts: little attempt is made to select tenants carefully in order to present a coordinated image to consumers, and there is no systematic effort to maintain the quality of the stores in the shopping center.

It was estimated that there were 18 agglomerations in 1972 that had embraced some of the American concepts and could be called shopping centers. Significantly, two-thirds of these centers have come into being since 1968. Shopping centers are being developed by such diverse groups as large department stores, real estate developers, large mass merchandising firms, private railroad companies, and groups of specialty stores specifically organized for this purpose. Financial institutions, notably insurance companies, are also becoming increasingly interested in diversification by developing shopping centers.

So far, the patterns of development have two primary forms. One is for a single department store or mass merchandising firm to become the primary developer; the other pattern is a consortium of diverse interest groups. Examples of the first type are the centers developed by Daiei and Seiyu. An example of the second is a center developed as Tamagawa Shopping Center in a suburb of Tokyo. It was organized and developed by a corporation sponsored by a major bank, a life insurance company, a leading real estate developer, and Takashimaya, a well-known department store.

Japanese shopping centers have several striking features. First, the Japanese centers are considerably smaller than their American counterparts. In fact, some have a total sales space of no more than 10,000 square meters. In terms of parking space, only four shopping centers have sufficient space to accommodate 700 automobiles. The total ground area of the outstanding Tamagawa Center, for example, is no larger than 215,000 square feet, with parking space for 1,000 automobiles.

Second, because of the security of land and consequent extremely high land cost, the Japanese version inevitably consists of multiple levels. Because of the widespread use of multiple level buildings, the total floor space is likely to exceed the size of the lot. The total floor space of the Tamagawa Center is almost twice the size of the lot itself. The center houses approximately 120 specialty stores and a large branch of the Takashimaya Department Store.

Third, unlike that of the United States, the primary mode of transportation used by customers is not the automobile, but rather various modes of public transportation. Particularly popular is the country's well-developed railroad network. It is estimated, for example, that to reach the Tamagawa Center 60 percent of its customers will travel to the center by train, 30 percent by automobile, and 10 percent on foot. Thus, ready access to public transportation will be an extremely important factor in the location decision.

As noted earlier, the development of shopping centers in Japan is still in the very early stage, and its success is yet to be tested. But given the very dynamic conditions now prevailing, it is expected that shopping centers will gain considerable popularity in the near future. According to one estimate, there will be 800 shopping centers by 1980. In fact, those firms that are currently constructing such centers are already searching for new sites for additional centers.

The creation of new centers is likely to take the form of cooperative action among a number of different institutions, including some that had never shown an interest in retailing before. The implications of such cooperation may very well go beyond the emergence of just another new marketing institution.

The following factors can be cited as the main reasons for the rapid growth of shopping centers. First, the rapid growth of suburbs in major urban areas has produced a huge impetus for them. As a consequence of the rapid trend toward urbanization, suburbs have developed around all major cities. The second factor is the rapid diffusion of automobiles. The availability of parking facilities in the shopping centers is particularly attractive in view of downtown congestion. Third, Japanese consumers are just beginning to experience one-stop shopping which the cluster of various stores makes possible.

GROWTH OF CONSUMER FINANCING

Another significant recent development in the Japanese marketing system which deserves our attention is the widespread use of consumer credit. Consumer financing existed in a rudimentary form in the prewar era, but only in the past several years has it shown tremendous growth.

Before World War I the use of consumer credit was associated with inferior products and did not enjoy wide social acceptance. In fact, installment purchase was confined to members of the very lowest social strata, but the general attitude toward this practice has undergone basic change in recent years.

As to the profile of consumers who make use of installment credit, the quarterly survey on consumption and savings conducted by the Economic Planning Agency provides us with excellent data. This survey is based on a carefully chosen nationwide sample of more than 5,000 households. As to the extent of consumer acceptance of installment credit, the latest report reveals that nearly 35 percent of the households surveyed were using consumer financing of some sort—which is certainly indicative of its wide acceptance. The average outstanding balance per household was roughly ¥27,600 or slightly less than $77, and new purchases on installment during the period amounted to about ¥15,000 or $42.

The survey also indicated the extent of installment purchases according to various income categories. As is evident in Table 4.13, the use of installment credit is widely diffused throughout the range of income classes. While the highest percentage of users was found in the middle income class (¥900,000 and ¥1.2 million), it is significant to note that almost 34 percent of households in the highest income class were also buying on installment credit.

Another indication of the acceptance of consumer credit is its use for purchase of expensive merchandise. Installment sales account for an important share of the total sales of these items. For example,

TABLE 4.13

Installment Credit According to Income Classes, 1970

Annual Income of Household (¥1,000)	Percentage of Households Using Credit	Average Outstanding Balance (¥1,000)	Average Purchase (¥1,000)
Under 300	17.8	3.2	2.6
300- 600	26.7	12.1	6.9
600- 900	36.0	20.4	11.7
900-1,200	38.6	32.2	18.9
1,200-1,500	37.6	32.2	18.3
1,500-1,800	33.6	26.6	17.8
Average	28.5	27.6	14.8

Source: Japan Economic Planning Agency, 1971.

about 58 percent of the total sales of household equipment, 36 percent of the sales of men's suits, and 33 percent of total bicycle sales are made in this manner. Details are presented in Table 4.14.

Retail sales made with consumer credit came to ¥70 billion in 1968, the last year for which statistics are available. Between 1962 and 1968, installment sales grew by 48 percent. In 1968, total installment sales accounted for slightly over 5 percent of total retail sales.

Consumer financing can be classified in a variety of ways. A convenient grouping is on the basis of sponsorship. According to this system there are four types: (1) programs sponsored by retailers, (2) the coupon system, (3) manufacturer-sponsored programs, and (4) programs sponsored by financial institutions. We shall consider each briefly.

1. The financing of sales by retail establishments is the oldest form of consumer credit in Japan. The total amount of consumer credit extended directly by retailers is difficult to estimate, but for certain types of products, such as furniture, jewelry, and musical instruments, it plays a major role. In retail-sponsored programs, retail stores themselves assume the risk, and they perform all the service functions associated with sales, including credit investigation, contract preparation, and collection. The terms of these programs vary according to product categories, but typically 20 percent of the purchase price is required for down payment, and the contract seldom exceeds one year.

2. A unique method of installment credit sales in Japan is what is commonly known as the coupon system. The objective of this program is to permit small independent stores to engage in installment credit sales. There are two types: one is a cooperative arrangement, organized and managed by the retailers themselves; the second is sponsored and managed by independent organizations that provide their services to retailers for a fee.

The first type is usually organized by neighborhood shopping centers or groups of specialty stores that are in the same line of business. They issue coupons to prospective purchasers, arrange for payment, and so on. There are some 1,200 such retailer-sponsored groups. The second type, of which there are possibly 90, is operated by a credit company, which issues coupons to qualified customers, who can use the coupons at any of the subscribing stores. The consumers then make regular monthly payments to the sponsoring organization, which in turn makes periodic settlements to its member stores. To facilitate credit investigation and collection, membership is drawn from organized groups, such as labor unions, other employee groups, and professional organizations.

The Ministry of International Trade and Industry reports that this form of installment sales has shown a steady growth in recent years, exceeding ¥150 billion annually, or 1.5 percent of total retail sales. Coupon programs are not nearly as important as installment sales programs sponsored by manufacturers or retailers, but for certain product lines they are extensively used. One example is men's clothing, with about 11 percent of total sales financed in this manner.

TABLE 4.14

Percentage of Total Sales Through
Installment Purchase of Selected Products, 1968

Item	Percentage of Total Sales
Household equipment	57.7
Men's suits	36.2
Household electrical appliances	34.1
Bicycles	33.4
Musical instruments	18.8
Bedding	16.1
Furniture	12.1

Source: Commercial Census, 1971.

3. The third general type are programs sponsored by major manufacturers of consumer durables, who now place major emphasis on installment sales as an effective marketing tool. Again, these programs are found in several principal forms. The first is a program whereby manufacturers, at their own risk, extend installment credit directly to consumers. Under this arrangement manufacturers undertake all the necessary functions associated with installment sales, including credit investigations and collection. This pattern is found primarily in the sale of products such as musical instruments and sewing machines, which are distributed through the manufacturer's own retail outlets.
   The second form is one in which dealers, on a fee basis, perform essential functions related to installment sales on behalf of the manufacturer. For reasons of cost and convenience, manufacturers generally prefer to let their dealers undertake credit investigation and collection, since these functions can best be performed at the level where sales are actually consummated. Even under this arrangement, manufacturers still assume financial as well as legal obligations.
   The third form is a program in which manufacturers supply most of the funds needed for financing installment sales, but their dealers perform all the necessary auxiliary functions, including the assumption of risk. This pattern has been followed in the sale of automobiles.
   In the fourth kind of program the manufacturers establish a subsidiary specializing in the extension of installment credit. These subsidiaries are generally known as installment credit companies, and they are either entirely financed by the parent company or jointly financed with affiliated wholesalers and retailers. This approach is most common in the sale of electric home appliances. For example, Matsushita Electric has a subsidiary specializing in installment financing, which, in turn, has some 72 satellite firms located throughout Japan. These companies do not engage in sales activities, but provide necessary financial and administrative support to dealers in making installment credit sales. The individual dealer turns over his installment sales contracts to the affiliated installment sales company in his territory, from which he receives immediate payment for the merchandise. Thus, as far as dealers are concerned, sales on installment are little different from cash sales.
   There is another type of manufacturer-oriented installment sales program that is basically different from those that have been described above. This is a plan whereby consumers make a series of regular prepayments to manufacturers or dealers before they actually receive the merchandise. In some cases payment must be completed, while in others a certain portion of the total price must be prepaid, before a purchaser can take possession of the goods.

The major inducement to consumers is a substantial discount in price. For obvious reasons this program is regulated, and only licensed manufacturers or dealers can engage in it. There are more than 230 authorized manufacturers and dealers serving some 10 million consumers, and the outstanding balance of such prepayment is estimated to run as high as ¥50 billion. This plan is particularly popular in the purchase of sewing machines, home appliances, and furniture.

4. The fourth form of consumer financing is one sponsored by financial institutions. Entry of financial institutions into the consumer credit field is a very recent phenomenon. Until a decade or so ago, the banks had almost completely confined their financing to large industrial clients. In the postwar development of consumer financing in Japan, financial institutions have played a key role as a major supplier of funds. As of December 1969 the outstanding balance of loans that financial institutions had extended to various types of firms engaged in installment sales amounted to ¥1,373 billion, representing roughly 3 percent of the total loan balance. The amount nearly doubled between 1965 and 1969. Approximately 80 percent of the outstanding loans have been made to automobile sales companies.

In addition to this indirect form of participation, commercial banks in recent years have become directly involved in consumer financing, particularly with installment credit. This has been a major innovation for Japanese banks, whcih traditionally confined their activities to large industrial clients. It was around 1960 when Japan's major city banks became interested in consumer financing. Japanese financial institutions entered into consumer financing for quite different reasons than those of their American counterparts. The latter entered this field in their search for more lucrative avenues for investing their funds, whereas Japanese city banks have done so for defensive reasons. Let me explain.

As a result of the very rapid development of securities markets in the late 1950s, Japan began to witness a major change in the flow of investment funds. Unlike in prewar Japan, ownership of securities became widely diffused among the people, thus competing with commercial banks for personal savings, which had been the prime source of funds for major banks. Between 1956 and 1961 the percentage of personal savings in the form of bank deposits declined from 62 percent to 55 percent, and during the same period the percentage of savings in the form of securities increased from 25 percent to nearly 32 percent. A relative decline of bank funds also can be seen from the fact that up until the late 1950s financial institutions supplied 90 percent of the financial requirements of Japanese industries, but by the early 1960s the percentage declined to about 76 percent. Particularly seriously affected were the city banks, Japan's major financial institutions, whose relative importance continuously declined during these years. The funds supplied by the city banks as a percentage of the total provided by all financial institutions declined from 54 percent in 1956 to 43 percent in 1962. This obviously had far-reaching implications for major commercial banks.

Faced with these situations, the city banks turned to consumer financing as a defensive strategy to attract a greater share of personal savings—an all-important source of funds. It was felt that consumer financing would be an effective tool to establish closer relationships with the masses and to popularize the city banks so that they would be in a better position to compete for personal savings. Another motivating force for the city banks was their view that entering into this field in cooperation with their major client firms would contribute to cementing their ties with them. This was one of the reasons why the city banks initially developed their installment programs in cooperation with specific large manufacturing enterprises. Sumitomo Bank, a well-known former Zaibatsu bank, pioneered this program in 1960 by developing a program for automobile financing in cooperation with the Prince Motor Company. Other city banks soon followed suit. The products commonly sold under this plan include automobiles, home appliances, and musical instruments.

In recent years, however, the banks have begun to make personal loans directly to consumers, not tied to the purchase of any specific product and without requiring the guarantee of a manufacturer. In some cases collateral is not even required. The bank has two types of consumer loans that are not tied to a particular firm or product. One type is based on a savings plan. To be eligible, customers must first make a deposit of a stipulated sum each month for ten consecutive months, and the maximum amount to be loaned under this plan is twenty times the monthly deposit. The other type is a straight personal loan, ranging in amount from ¥30,000 to ¥2 million. Repayments are made on a monthly installment basis for a maximum of three years. The bank loans up to ¥1 million without security, but does require two cosigners, who must guarantee the loan.

At the time of this writing, 12 of the 13 city banks were engaged in consumer financing. With the entry of the major city banks into the consumer financing field, other types of financial institutions quickly followed their example. Now virtually all 63 provincial banks are engaged in consumer financing, and others, such as trust companies, long-term credit banks, mutual loan and saving banks, and credit associations, have also entered this field.

From a rather modest beginning, financial institutions have entered the consumer financing field at a very rapid rate. Particularly noteworthy are the inroads made by the provincial banks. The outstanding balance of installment credit extended by provincial banks accounted for roughly 42 percent of total consumer installment loans. Aware of further growth opportunities, the banks are increasing their commitments to consumer financing. A number of city and provincial banks have established a separate organizational unit specializing in consumer financing.

Outstanding consumer credit extended by the commercial banks directly to consumers exceeds ¥1.5 trillion, and amounts to roughly 2.6 percent of total consumer credit. If the loans extended to automobile purchasers and loans made to retail outlets to finance their installment sales are included, the total loans extended by the commercial banks exceed ¥3 trillion, accounting for over 5 percent of the total loans extended.

CHAPTER 5

JAPANESE TRADING COMPANIES

The Japanese trading company is a unique business institution in the world today and has no parallel among trading firms of the past in other countries. American businessmen, though quite familiar with its existence, seldom have a complete picture of what the trading company is. Because of its singular importance in Japan's domestic and international business, some understanding of a trading company's function is vitally important to those interested in dealing with Japan. Such an understanding of the trading company is critical to the American businessman in several ways. First, the trading company can be highly useful in distributing products in Japan. Trading companies, as we shall see later, are responsible for a major share of Japan's imports and, because of its extensive international network, the trading company could be an excellent agent for the American firms interested in exporting their products to Japan.

Second, the trading company can be a suitable partner in joint ventures for the American firm wishing to establish a sales or manufacturing subsidiary in Japan. Because of its excellent standing in the business community, close connections with the city banks, and availability of first-rate managerial resources, the trading company is in an excellent position to provide a strong impetus to a joint venture.

Third, the trading company's worldwide network can be profitably mobilized by American companies in reaching other markets in the world. The trading company is becoming increasingly interested in promoting trade outside of Japan. The so-called third country trade (trade between countries other than Japan) is still negligible, but a growing number of American corporations, particularly smaller companies, are becoming increasingly interested in having the Japanese trading company perform distribution functions in a number of foreign markets.

Finally, the trading company can be a powerful competitor for the American companies operating in Japan. The trading company is so intricately involved in Japanese marketing operations that it is likely to pose a serious competitive threat in a number of product categories.

There are two central characteristics of a trading company that are impressive. The first is their massive size. The combined sales figures of the ten largest trading companies provide telling evidence of their great size—they represent slightly over a quarter of Japan's total GNP. The second characteristic is the diversity of their operations. The time has passed when the trading company confined its operations to just traditional trading; it now is involved in resource development, manufacturing, mining, urban and regional development, and a number of service industries as well.

There are several thousand trading companies in Japan, but the general trading company, known as the "sogo shosha," is the most important type. There are ten leading sogo shosha in Japan, which are by far the most influential in the entire sector. In this chapter we shall confine our analysis to these trading companies.

The scale of operations of a typical sogo shosha is something like the following: it has a sales volume of $5 or $6 billion and, as already noted, is engaged in a wide variety of activities. It has a staff of 10,000 or more, located in 50 domestic offices and 80 overseas branches and subsidiaries. Each major trading company, as we shall see later, has close ties with one or more of the major city banks and with a group of large and small manufacturing firms.

EVOLUTION

In order to understand the nature of the trading company, we must understand its evolution. The trading company is a product of Japan's unique economic and cultural system. It was born out of the rather peculiar set of circumstances under which Japan's industrialization was undertaken.

The trading companies may be categorized into three types. One type is Zaibatsu based and is represented by the two giant firms of Mitsui and Mitsubishi; the second type are those firms with origins in the textile business; and the third type started in the steel industry. We shall briefly trace the origins of each.

In the first category, the Mitsui Trading Company is the most outstanding. By the time of the Meiji Restoration (1868), the Mitsui family had built a thriving commercial business. It established its trading arm in 1878, in part to respond to the needs of a growing foreign trade. Up until then, nearly all such activities had been controlled by foreigners, who exploited Japanese ignorance of how to transact foreign business. A few years later, the Mitsubishi Zaibatsu also established its trading arm. Each of these trading companies later came to occupy a central position in its respective Zaibatsu. Subsequently, as they actively sought to diversify into mining and manufacturing, the functions of the Zaibatsu companies became increasingly important and these companies became the leaders of Japan's industrialization. Rapid growth and diversification of the Zaibatsu, in turn, gave further impetus to the development of the trading companies. Not only had they built up an extensive manufacturing and marketing network in Japan, they had also gained the dominant position in foreign trade. As the Zaibatsu became firmly established in the heavy industries and gained dominance over the Japanese financial sector, the trading companies established virtual monopolies over the distribution of a number of key commodities, such as sugar, petroleum, soybeans, and fertilizer. Moreover, the trading companies, through their extensive network in the international scene, were instrumental in introducing new technologies useful for Japan's further development. In the process, the two trading companies had achieved preeminence in Japanese industry. By the early 1930s, Mitsui Trading Company alone was responsible for roughly 32 percent of the nation's total foreign trade.

The second of the types of trading companies, those specializing in the textile field, also began in the late 1800s with the development of the cotton-spinning industry in Japan. The need to procure raw cotton from foreign sources gave rise to trading companies specializing in that field. The cotton-spinning industry soon developed sufficiently to be able to produce for export markets; and the trading companies that had been developed in the first place to handle cotton procurement became the export agents for cotton textiles. These trading companies were based in Osaka, which has been the center of the nation's textile industry for the past century. C. Itoh and Marubeni, now the third and fourth largest trading companies, began in this field.

The third type of trading company can trace its origins to the birth of the steel industry in Japan. In the early days of the nation's industrialization, Japan had to depend on foreign sources for iron and steel, and a few trading companies specializing in steel products emerged. When the nation's first steel mill was established by the government in 1901, primarily to meet the rapidly growing demand for military requirements, the surplus was sold to civilians. Subsequently, several privately-owned steel mills were created, increasing the need for trading companies to procure iron ores overseas and to distribute the end products. This process gave rise to a half-dozen powerful trading companies in this field. Both Nisho-Iwai and Ataka, the fifth and sixth largest trading firms at present, had their beginnings in this field. Thus, the trading company gained prominence in the prewar era, and provided vital functions in Japan's industrialization.

STRUCTURE

In the immediate aftermath of World War II, the Zaibatsu were broken up. In the process, the two powerful trading companies, Mitsui and Mitsubishi, were dissolved into numerous small units, the former being fragmented into 123 smaller companies. Meantime, capitalizing on the vacuum created by the dissolution of these two giant firms, the five leading firms specializing in the textile field achieved phenomenal growth. The Korean War provided a strong impetus. It gave an excellent opportunity for the non-Zaibatsu trading firms to diversify out of their traditional fields of textiles and steel into other fields, such as machinery, metals, and chemicals.

Shortly after Japan regained her independence in the early 1950s, the Zaibatsu began to reemerge, though in a considerably altered form. The two trading companies, Mitsui and Mitsubishi, through successive consolidations, became united as one company. Once they were, it did not take these companies long to regain their prewar leadership and once again achieve their dominant positions. Subsequently, Mitsui and Mitsubishi, being the largest trading companies in Japan, have been competing for first place.

Significant changes have also occurred among the major non-Zaibatsu firms. For one thing, they have become highly diversified. For example, C. Itoh and Marubeni, the two major trading companies that had once specialized in textiles, have now become totally diversified firms. In C. Itoh, textile products are responsible for only a third of the total business; in Marubeni, the proportion is even less, accounting for slightly over 20 percent of its total business.

In the second significant postwar development, the character of trading companies has undergone equally important changes. They have expanded considerably in their nontrading activities. In the early 1960s the trading company in its traditional form faced a serious crisis. The relative importance of its traditional role in the field of trading declined and the future of the trading company was in doubt. Recognizing the crisis, the major trading companies have undergone major reorganizations and have attempted to diversify into new areas of activity. Indeed, the trading companies have moved quickly and have responded extremely well to meet the changing situation.

Another significant development is the mergers among major non-Zaibatsu trading companies. The two most noteworthy of these were between Nissho and Iwai, and between Kanematsu and Gosho. Other merger possibilities have been explored, but not implemented. The merger of Nissho and Iwai is particularly revealing in indicating the close relationship that exists between manufacturing and trading companies. This consolidation came about primarily as a result of the merger of the two largest steel mills, Yawata and Fuji, which, respectively, the two trading companies served.

Latest commercial statistics list almost 7,000 trading companies in Japan. The sales of the trading companies amounted to $82 billion, roughly half of the nation's GNP. This figure alone is telling evidence of the status that trading companies occupy in Japan. Even more significant is the fact that a very small number of extremely large trading companies account for the bulk of the sales volume. The ten largest companies are responsible for 58 percent of total sales. The fifteen second largest companies account for another 10 percent of the total business. Thus, the largest twenty-five companies are responsible for nearly 70 percent of the total business done by trading companies. The ten major corporations will be listed in Table 5.1.

There are several important characteristics that distinguish these ten dominant firms from the rest. First, as has been mentioned, they are extremely large. The combined sales volume of the ten firms is no less than $48 billion, comparable roughly to a quarter of the nation's GNP. The largest four alone are responsible for over

TABLE 5.1

The Ten Largest Trading Companies, 1971

Name	Total Sales (¥ million)	Net Profit (¥ million)	Number of Employees
Mitsubishi Shoji	4,621,000	12,951	9,973
Mitsui Bussan	4,370,000	8,117	13,208
Marubeni	3,030,000	5,000	7,976
M. C. Itoh	2,847,000	8,684	7,263
Sumilomo Shoji	2,125,000	3,293	6,475
Nisho Iwai	2,028,000	2,600	7,154
Tomen	1,415,000	1,800	4,322
Kanemasu-Gosho	1,040,000	1,055	3,565
Ataka	1,000,000	1,455	3,631
Nichimen	969,000	1,490	3,924

Source: Annual reports of the companies.

12 percent of the nation's total wholesale volume. They are dominant in the nation's international trade as well. The Big Ten are responsible for 47 percent of the export trade of Japan and 68 percent of her total imports. The largest four alone account for 33 percent of exports and 40 percent of imports.

The relative size of trading companies can be seen by noting that the total sales of Mitsubishi Trading Company are three times the sales of Shin Nihon Seitsu, the largest manufacturing firm in Japan. Naturally, the sales volume of trading firms and manufacturing companies are not directly comparable; but nevertheless the figures indicate the enormous size of a major trading company.

The second notable feature of the Big Ten is the diversity of their activities. As we shall see later, in addition to ordinary trading, their activities range from resource exploration to development of recreational facilities. Even the commodities handled cover a wide range. "From noodles to missiles," a phrase often used to describe the diversity of the products carried by the trading companies, is indeed an accurate one. The number of items handled by these major trading companies exceeds 10,000.

The third major characteristic is their ability to mobilize huge financial resources. It is not without reason that the two largest trading companies, Mitsui and Mitsubishi, boast of the largest amount of capital of any Japanese corporation.

The fourth characteristic is that they enjoy international networks. They have been serving as the eyes and ears of Japan's major manufacturers as well as of smaller firms for nearly a century. The leading trading companies have branches, offices, and representatives throughout the world. The organization of a trading company is such as to allow close integration of activities among branches and offices that are geographically scattered.

The last, but not the least, important factor is their worldwide reputation. The major trading companies are world renowned. Virtually anywhere in the world the names of Mitsui, Mitsubishi, and Marubeni enjoy a high degree of credit worthiness. This makes it possible for each new branch or subsidiary to mobilize worldwide financial resources as well as to cultivate new customers.

FUNCTIONS

What functions do the sogo shosha, or general trading companies, perform? Their strength is not derived from performing any single function, but from their ability to supply a number of functions for one client. Their role as a synergetic force is their secret of success. While recognizing this fact, let us look at each of the major functions and consider how they are combined to maximize total impact.

The most basic function of trading companies, as the name implies, is the trading of commodities. Trading involves both domestic and foreign trade in approximately equal amounts. The commodities handled, as discussed earlier, are highly varied. The percentage breakdown by product categories of the total transactions made by the ten leading companies is roughly as follows:

iron & steel	23%
machinery & equipment	17
foodstuffs	13
textiles	16
nonferrous metals	8
chemicals	7
oil	4
miscellaneous goods	12
	100%

Most of the goods handled by trading companies have two major characteristics. One is that they are handled in bulk. The other is that they tend not to be technically oriented. When selling items with significant degrees of technical complexity, such as machinery and equipment, which tend to be well developed technically, a trading company must draw on the support of a manufacturing company. Within trading functions, there are many subcomponents such as assuming credit risk, performing storage functions, and furnishing transportation. Trading companies are not brokers or commission merchants, but they take over titles to goods handled and, in that sense, assume all of the risks that are routinely associated with commercial transactions.

Another highly useful subfunction that the trading company performs is its ability to develop suppliers, whether foreign or domestic. These efforts range from large-scale transactions, involving long-term contracts and a large capital outlay, to relatively small-scale efforts with limited commitments. Examples of large-scale projects are to be found in the exploration and development of crude oil and mineral resources. Currently there are some thirty separate projects for exploration and development of crude oil sources and, almost without exception, major trading companies have some equity participation in these ventures. Virtually all the iron ore needed by Japanese steel mills is provided by trading companies. Given the tremendous growth in the Japanese steel industry during the last decade, its requirement for iron ore has soared; between 1966 and 1971 the iron ore consumed by the Japanese steel industry increased from slightly over 21 million tons to over 117 million tons. Such a rapid increase in the demand for iron ore has compelled the trading companies to undertake source development. The two giant trading firms, Mitsui and Mitsubishi, supply nearly 50 percent of the iron ore required in Japan.

The effort of trading companies to engage in source development goes far beyond the natural resources. In fact, such services are found in a number of merchandise categories. This is particularly the case when products are manufactured by a large number of small enterprises. Japan is well known for the overwhelming dominance of small enterprises (at least in number), and trading companies work closely with these firms to provide marketing and financing functions for them. The large trading company has been credited with providing an important link between the myriads of small manufacturers and the large manufacturers, and with making it possible for small firms to export their products.

By achieving control over supply sources, and by virtually turning them into their captive suppliers, trading companies can reap considerable benefits. The typical manner by which they do so is not through outright ownership but through extension of credit, through management and technical assistance and, most importantly, through providing outlets for their products. Such an organizational function is a forte of the large trading company.

Another activity that closely relates to the trading functions is the well-established network of marketing channels through controlled outlets which the major trading companies have developed. Throughout the history of trading companies, they have sought, usually successfully, to establish downward vertical control over distributors and wholesalers. Significantly, however, until very recently trading companies' control over marketing intermediaries had usually stopped at the wholesale level, and had not penetrated into the retail level. Until the advent of mass merchandising firms, retail units were too small to make the involvement of trading companies feasible. In extending their control over wholesalers and distributors, trading companies have essentially resorted to the same methods they used with manufacturers. Here again, credit extension is the critical element. Also, in some cases, supply sources are so tightly controlled that it is all but impossible for distributors to buy except through trading companies.

In addition to those tasks already mentioned, trading companies perform a variety of other functions which support normal trading activities, including warehousing, transportation and storage. Typically, a large trading company has a myriad of subsidiaries, affiliate firms, or subcontractors which perform these auxiliary services.

Development of New Businesses

In addition to trading in established commodities such as textiles, iron, nonferrous metals, and foods, trading companies have been relentlessly seeking opportunities for diversification into other fields. Not only have they added new product lines, but what is even more important, they have assumed the role of developing new business ventures in a number of fields. There are a number of reasons for this. For one thing, trading companies must expand beyond their traditional lines of business of trading in basic commodities. The Japanese economy is becoming highly capital intensive and technically oriented. Trading companies cannot hope to maintain their viability by simply confining their activities to trading in low technology-oriented fields.

Second, in entering new business ventures, trading companies seek to supply the new company with needed commodities, raw materials, or machinery and equipment. For example, when the trading company invests in a project to explore and develop crude oil overseas, it generally attempts to become the main supplier of necessary equipment and machinery to the new company. It is often stated, perhaps not inaccurately, that the most immediate incentive for trading companies to enter new business ventures is to be able to increase their trade volume by supplying the venture—the profit from that venture itself is only secondary.

The third benefit to be derived from entering a new venture is that the trading company can enhance its ties with other corporations. Seldom does a trading company enter a new field alone. It generally forms a joint venture, or consortium, with other corporations. This helps establish or strengthen its relationship with other companies, which often produces important side benefits, such as subsequent opportunities for important new ventures. While trading companies seldom make a large-scale entry into a new field alone, they do take the initiative. They identify new opportunities, search for partners, investigate the market, formulate entry strategies, participate in fund raising, provide management know-how, and so on. The trading company becomes the focal point in the new venture management. Of course, considerable risk is associated with such a role. Understandably, many of the potential ideas are never realized; some fall by the wayside as the plans become more concrete. But if the venture is successful, the payoff is great.

Development of new ventures takes on a wide variety of forms. One popular form is a joint venture with foreign companies. There, trading companies have some decided advantages. They serve a large number of foreign firms, as the distributors of their products in Japan, and it is only a natural step for the foreign firms to consider entering into joint ventures in Japan, either to strengthen their position in the existing product lines or to enter a new field. The trading company is also able to identify promising business opportunities through its international network. It is familiar with current business trends, including those which have proved to be successful in other parts of the world, and is in an excellent position to identify new business opportunities that may be attractive to Japan.

Also, given their strength in the domestic market, major trading companies receive constant inquiries from foreign firms interested in penetrating the Japanese market. Some of the new businesses that have emerged through joint ventures with foreign firms include computer softwares, leasing and franchising chains of fast foods. Entry into new fields through joint ventures with foreign firms has been attractive to both sides. Through this method trading companies lacking skills and know-how in a particular field were able to move into that field very quickly. To foreign companies, trading companies are excellent partners, because of their excellent knowledge of the market, financial power, and first-rate managerial competence. However, the major thrusts thus far for entering new fields have usually taken the form of collaboration with other large Japanese firms.

New fields entered by major trading companies in recent years include urban and regional development, the leisure industry, the housing industry, and health care. These new fields entered by trading companies have several common features. First, they have considerable growth possibilities and involve potentially large markets. Second, they require considerable capital commitment. Third, the fields are so complex from a technical and managerial standpoint and so large that no single company can undertake them by itself; they require a focal point or a coordinating organization. The trading company has performed this vital organizational function and is, therefore, often referred to as a "organizer."

Table 5.2 presents new fields which major Japanese corporations, including the trading companies, are planning to enter, and it is noteworthy that the four leading trading companies, Mitsubishi Shoji, Mitsui Bassa, C. Itoh, and Marubeni, are seeking entry into all of the fields indicated.

We have briefly examined the functions of trading companies. The traditional functions of trading companies still occupy a central position in their activities. A trading company's major roles have been to extend credit, develop markets, nurture suppliers, develop a network of controlled distributors, assume risk, and perform supportive services.

The nontrading activities are becoming increasingly important. Entry into new growth fields has been a central concern. The fields

TABLE 5.2

The Major Companies of Japan and the New
Industries Each Plans to Enter

Company	Information	Housing	Regional Dev.	Oceanography	Space	Leisure	Atomic Energy	Medicine	Automation	Defense	Transportation	Distribution	Services
Yawata Iron & Steel		*		*			*						
Mitsubishi Heavy			*	*	*		*				*	*	
Fuji Iron & Steel		*	*	*									
IHI		*		*	*		*			*	*	*	
Furukawa Electric	*	*					*						
Sumitomo Electric	*	*	*				*						
Hitachi	*	*	*				*	*	*				
Toshiba Electric	*	*	*	*	*		*	*	*				
Matsushita Electric	*		*	*									
Toyota Motors			*						*		*		
Nissan Motors	*				*					*			
Nippon Oil			*	*			*						
Idemitsu Oil			*	*							*		
Mitsubishi Chemical		*	*	*			*	*					
Mitsui Toatsu Chemical		*							*		*		
Toray	*	*	*										
Teijin		*		*				*					*
Jujo Paper	*	*				*	*		*				
Oji Paper	*	*	*								*		
Dainippon Printing	*	*				*							*
Toppan Printing	*	*											*
Tokyo Electric Power				*			*						
Kansai Electric Power	*		*	*			*						
Kinki Nippon RR		*				*					*		*
Kashima Construction		*	*				*	*					
Takenaka Engineering	*	*	*	*			*	*			*		*
Mitsubishi Shoji	*	*	*	*	*	*	*	*	*	*	*	*	*
Mitsui & Co.	*	*	*	*	*	*	*	*	*	*	*	*	*
Marubeni Iida	*	*	*	*	*	*	*	*	*	*	*	*	*
C. Itoh	*	*	*	*	*	*	*	*	*	*	*	*	*

Source: Kyosuke Arita, <u>Sogo Shosha</u>, (Tokyo, Nippon Keizai Shimbunsha, 7th ed., 1971) p. 166.

entered cut across all major industrial sectors—extractive, manufacturing, and services. Here the major role of the trading company has been that of an innovative organizer, entrepreneur, planner, and manager. Indeed, the major trading companies have been the prime movers in venture businesses in Japan.

THE SOURCES OF TRADING COMPANIES' STRENGTH

The foregoing examination clearly points out that trading companies occupy an important position in the Japanese economy. They are a unique institution that has no close parallel elsewhere. And what are their main strengths?

The Benefits of Group Affiliation

When the trading company was created, as we have seen, it was not as an entity by itself, but as an element in a larger commercial, financial, and industrial system. Particularly, the two dominant trading companies, Mitsui and Mitsubishi, were organized within the framework of giant Zaibatsu groups, and in the respective groups each has always held considerable influence.

Zaibatsu groups, though destroyed in the immediate aftermath of the war, have emerged again in the postwar period, although in an altered form. The disappearance of the holding companies, an important hallmark of the prewar Zaibatsu, has even strengthened the position of trading companies in the group. Particularly in the Mitsubishi and Mitsui groups, trading companies now occupy a central leadership role. The fact that the major trading companies are a part of giant enterprise groups has several important benefits. For one thing, an important share of their business comes directly from within the groups. The Mitsubishi group, for example, consists of two dozen or so corporations in which each is a leader in its respective field, and has a large number of subsidiaries and affiliated companies of its own. The Mitsubishi Trading Company derives roughly 30 percent of its total sales from transactions within the group. Even the Mitsui group, whose position as a whole has suffered a decline in the postwar decades, and which is known for rather weak ties, derives over 20 percent of its total sales from intragroup transactions.

C. Itoh and Marubeni had not belonged to a traditional Zaibatsu group, but each, in cooperation with major city banks, has developed groups of its own, and each does a substantial amount of business within its own group.

Another benefit that trading companies derive from group affiliation is the ability to mobilize these corporations for a common project. Sister corporations look to trading companies for new business opportunities and, if approached by the trading company, there is a good chance that they will cooperate and join forces with it. The trading company's ready access to a large number of well-established and highly reputable corporations certainly facilitates its entry into new fields. Of course, these present groups are far less cohesive than were the previous Zaibatsu. Without the holding company at the helm, and with only limited interlocking of stock ownership and directorates, the relationship is a rather fluid one. Thus, no trading company can claim an exclusive relationship with any of its sister firms in the same group. In fact, a number of ventures are organized by joint efforts of companies cutting across the traditional Zaibatsu boundaries. Nevertheless, these group ties still exist and certainly do play an important role.

International Information Network

The second major strength of the trading company is derived from its information network. Trading companies served as eyes and ears for Japan in the early days of the country's industrialization. Through their extensive international networks, they identified new products and technologies for Japan and provided market information to the manufacturers of export goods. The international network of a trading company is indeed a unique feature. Major trading companies maintain a large number of branches and offices throughout the world, which are staffed by Japanese and local citizens and are connected to each other by telecommunication systems. Mitsui Trading Company has a network of over 100 offices and branches in the world. Nearly 1,000 employees of Mitsui are assigned to these foreign offices, assisted by some 2,000 local employees. Mitsubishi's international network is equally impressive. Mitsubishi International Corporation, a wholly owned U.S. subsidiary of the corporation, is a major corporation in its own right, with annual sales approaching $3 billion. In the United States alone Mitsubishi maintains six branches, each of which is of substantial size.

These foreign offices serve a variety of purposes. The most important, of course, is their trading function. It is through these offices that most of the day-to-day transactions, customer contacts, and market development are accomplished. But in addition to these regular activities, they perform useful services of identifying new technologies, new markets, new products, and new business partners. Their ability to obtain and process information is quite impressive.

Excellence in Management

Still another strength of the trading company is its excellent management. Over the years, the major trading companies have been successful in building up a cadre of first-rate managers. Major trading companies enjoy high prestige in Japan and are able to attract the best graduates of Japan's leading universities. Trading companies are among the most highly preferred places of employment. Also, over the years they have developed a large number of specialties in certain commodities, industries, and geographic areas. There is virtually no skill trading companies lack. The devoted management, the quality of their staffs and their expert knowledge and experience are major assets of Japan's large trading companies.

Financial Services

The fourth major strength of the trading company is its financial capabilities. In fact, the claim is often made that the financial muscle of a trading company is the single most important asset in making it an extremely powerful institution.

It is well known that Japanese corporations place heavy reliance on debt. Indeed, the debt-equity ratio in a typical Japanese corporation seems astonishingly high to those whose experience is with U.S. firms and who are unfamiliar with the Japanese scene. Debts take two major forms: one is short- and long-term loans; the other is regular trade credit. In the latter, trading companies perform a very important service. The amount of credit extended by leading trading companies is staggering. The ten largest companies, for example, extended about $32 billion worth of trade credit to their customers in the form of accounts or notes receivable in a single recent year. This amount is equivalent to roughly one-sixth of the total loans extended by all banks in Japan. Almost without exception, sales by trading companies are transacted through credit as a part of the service a trading company is expected to provide. Thus, it is not surprising that trading companies, on the average, have trade credit extended that is equivalent to three or four months' sales.

In addition to this extensive financing, trading companies have a substantial commitment in the form of investments. For example, in March 1972, the ten major trading companies had over $3.5 billion invested. These investments take a wide range of forms, from participation in the development of raw materials to investment in small subcontractors. Approximately 15 percent of this investment is in their subsidiaries, which operate as a part of the total corporation. Both in relative and absolute terms, trading companies' investment in subsidiaries has increased significantly over the last decade.

In addition to making direct investments or loans, trading companies guarantee loans on behalf of their customers and related firms. Their ability to extend loans, to make investments, and to guarantee loans, has given them an enormous competitive advantage over their suppliers as well as their customers.

Where do the trading companies obtain their funds? They, too, rely heavily on debt sources. The total net working capital of the ten largest trading companies is roughly ¥2,513 billion, or roughly $9.5 billion, which is about ten times the combined net worth of these companies. Furthermore, these ten companies in aggregate had total outstanding loans of ¥3,961 billion or $15 billion, making their average debt-to-equity ratio an astonishing fifteen to one. They meet these large fund requirements primarily through bank loans; roughly 27 percent comes from long-term loans, 40 percent from short-term loans, and the rest comes from commercial bills discounted at the banks. Of course, given Japanese tradition, the distinction between long- and short-term loans is by no means clear-cut.

The large-scale borrowing from commercial banks makes major trading companies the heaviest debtors in Japan by far. In fact, in all ten trading companies the interest payments are higher than the operating profit. For the second half of 1971, for example, the net operating profit of the ten largest trading companies was reported to be ¥98 billion; the total interest paid was ¥123 billion.

The Mitsubishi Trading Company, during that period, had a net operating profit of ¥22 billion and paid out ¥28 billion in interest. Mitsui's case is even more dramatic. Their net profit was approximately the same as that of the Mitsubishi, but the company paid out ¥44 billion in interest!

Over the years the trading companies and banks have developed a very close working relationship. Here we need to examine the unique relationship that has evolved between the large trading companies and the major city banks in Japan, for it has several important implications. Throughout the postwar decades, for a variety of reasons, the major city banks have sought to establish close ties with leading trading companies. In return, trading companies have enjoyed ready access to capital from city banks at very attractive rates. Thus, the banks and trading companies had a clear mutuality of interest.

For one thing, trading companies that are members of a former Zaibatsu group, notably Mitsui, Mitsubishi, and Sumitomo, obviously enjoy close ties with financial institutions that belong to the same group, thus deriving enormous benefits by being part of a powerful enterprise. For non-Zaibatsu trading companies, such as C. Itoh or Marubeni, the situation is not very different. Major city banks are anxious to build their enterprise groups and need collaborators;

indeed, in such endeavors trading company participation is almost essential. Thus, Marubeni occupies an important position in the Fuyo group organized around the Fuji Bank and C. Itoh, where the relationship is less clear-cut, and maintains a close relationship with two major city banks.

The city banks, eager to improve their positions, compete vigorously to extend favorable credit to major trading companies. Much like trading companies themselves, the city banks have been engaged in aggressive competition for deposits. From that point of view, trading companies constitute excellent clients because of their sheer volume of business. Also, at one time the city banks were anxious to handle foreign exchange transactions for the trading companies to strengthen their position in this field; for the amount of foreign exchange handled was an important consideration in obtaining approval to open new foreign branches and offices from the Ministry of Finance.

For all these reasons, city banks have favored trading companies in extending loans at attractive interest rates. In this process, a tacit understanding between the banks and trading companies emerged. City banks make large loans to trading companies which, in turn, and at their own risk, "retail" the funds to both large and small enterprises. In effect, the banks use the trading companies to screen loans to small enterprises.

The trading company with its size, diversification, and reputation represents an excellent credit risk. The city bank's preference for dealing with the trading companies is well justified when the high failure rate of small enterprises is considered. In 1971 alone, there were over 9,000 bankruptcies, the overwhelming majority involving small or medium-sized enterprises. The trading company can, of course, use the funds to its own advantage in many ways that the banks cannot. Thus, the trading companies have been willing to assume the risk, and have been serving as a financial intermediary between the major city banks and large, and particularly a myriad of small, enterprises. While this cozy relationship has been gradually ending in recent years, as we shall see later, it has been tremendously effective and beneficial for all concerned.

FINANCIAL PERFORMANCE

How good is the performance of major trading companies ? Here, the answer depends largely on the criteria used. Judged by profit to sales ratio, profitability of trading companies looks very poor indeed. The average ratio of net profit (after taxes) to sales of Japan's four largest trading companies stands at about 0.2 percent.

The ratio of profit to total capital employed is also low. For example, the ratios for Mitsubishi and Mitsui are 0.6 and 0.5 percent, respectively. The major reason for that is the very low gross profit margin. The margin is seldom over 5 percent and, in large-volume transactions, it can be as low as 2 percent.

Trading companies are, however, quite profitable when they are measured by a return on equity. The average for the ten largest firms for 1971 was 27 percent. Table 5.3 indicates an interesting comparison of return on investment of the average of the Big Ten trading companies with that of Hitachi, a large manufacturing firm.

In examining the performance of major trading companies, it is clear that the Big Ten enjoy significant economies of scale. Their average cost of selling, general, and administrative expenses is only approximately 1.4 percent of their sales revenues, as demonstrated in Table 5.4. The same ratio can be as high as 25 percent for small enterprises. In fact, this extremely low operating cost is the most critical element preventing manufacturing firms from entering the trading business themselves. Obviously, companies with relatively small transaction volumes must earn a higher gross margin in order

TABLE 5.3

Return on Investment
(Before Taxes) for
Six-Month Term Ending March 1972
(in percentages)

	Ten Largest Trading Companies	Hitachi
Return of capital employed	2.50	8.0
Impact on nonoperating items (excluding interest expense)	2.60	0.72
Impact of nonfinancial capital	4.40	4.36
Return on investment	9.49	12.3
Impact of external borrowings (effect of interest expenses)	7.9	4.90
	17.5	6.7
(effect of financial leverage)	25.4	11.6
Return on shareholders' equity	27.1	19.0

Source: Company records.

TABLE 5.4

Selling, General, and Administrative Expenses of
the Ten Leading Trading Companies as a
Percentage of Sales Revenues, 1969-70

Companies	Second Half of 1969	First Half of 1970	Second Half of 1970
Mitsubishi	1.05	1.07	1.11
Mitsui	1.08	1.15	1.13
Marubeni	1.53	1.35	1.41
C. Itoh	1.11	1.14	1.10
Nissho	1.75	1.65	1.56
Sumitomo	2.53	2.27	2.43
Tomen	1.19	1.30	1.43
Nichimen	1.30	1.41	1.50
Kanematsu	1.95	1.89	1.75
Ataka	1.80	1.78	1.74
Average	1.39	1.38	1.39

Source: Annual reports of the companies.

to compensate for high operating costs. Trading firms' gross margin rates are largely determined by their levels of operating costs which, in turn, are determined by their size.

The ten leading trading companies have shown a rapid rate of growth during the past decade. The ten companies on the average grew in their sales volume by 17.1 percent annually, exceeding the growth rate of the GNP during the same period. The export transactions handled by these firms grew by 17 percent, and imports by 15 percent annually for the past decade. In both exports and imports the growth rate for the ten leading firms exceeded the rate for the entire nation for the same period.

It is significant, however, that the growth rate varied considerably among the ten firms. A key variable as demonstrated in Figure 5.1 is the kind of merchandise handled. Sumitomo Shoji, with the largest component of heavy industrial goods, recorded the highest growth rate, whereas the firms with a larger share of textiles and foodstuffs showed the lowest rate of growth.

FIGURE 5.1

Annual Growth Rate of the Ten Large Leading Trading Companies
by Type of Commodities Handled, 1970
(in percentages)

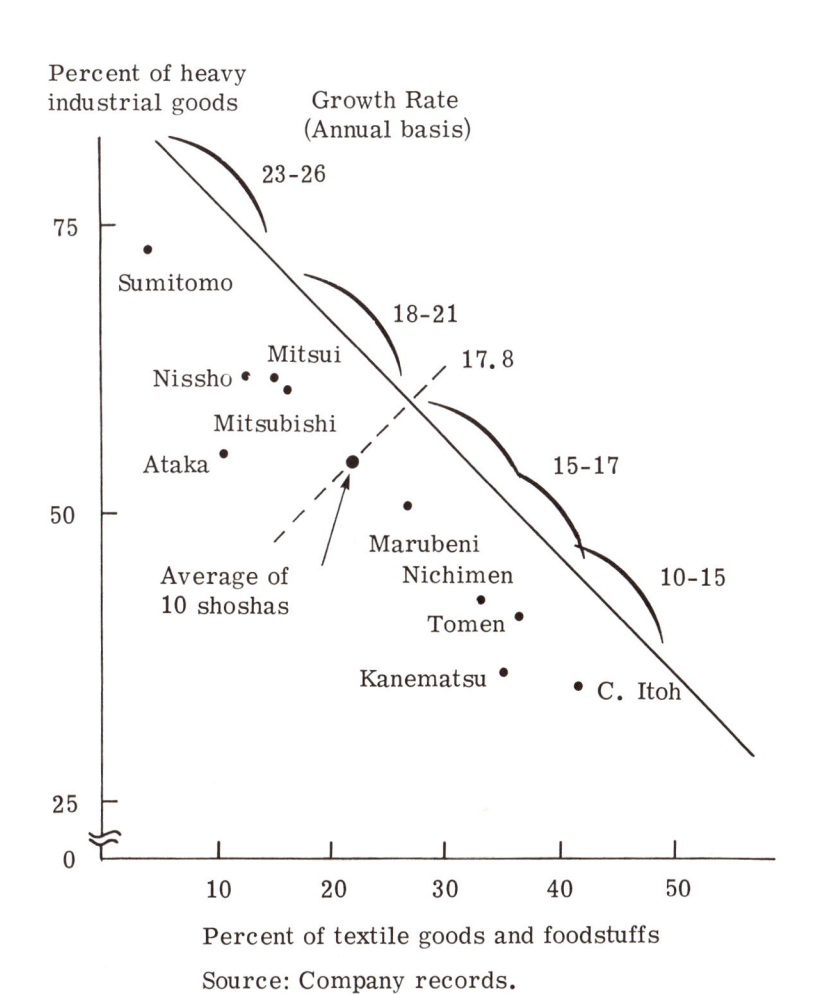

Percent of heavy industrial goods / Growth Rate (Annual basis)

- 23-26
- 18-21
- 17.8
- 15-17
- 10-15

Companies plotted: Sumitomo, Nissho, Mitsui, Mitsubishi, Ataka, Marubeni, Nichimen, Tomen, Kanematsu, C. Itoh, Average of 10 shoshas

Y-axis: 75, 50, 25, 0
X-axis: 10, 20, 30, 40, 50 — Percent of textile goods and foodstuffs

Source: Company records.

ENTRY INTO THE RETAIL SECTOR

One of the major activities that trading companies have undertaken in recent years is to enter the retail market. Up until recently they had confined their activities to the wholesale sector. With the advent of the mass market, and the development of mass merchandising firms, major trading companies have shown a growing interest in this area and have attempted to enter the field with varying success.

First, a number of major trading companies, having seen promising opportunities in mass merchandising, have entered this field, primarily in the form of supermarkets. This is a rather remarkable departure from the past pattern, since traditionally trading firms had not engaged in retailing activities themselves. As early as 1963 Sumitomo Trading Company planned to establish a supermarket chain in Japan jointly with Safeway of the United States. Because of stiff opposition from independent local retailers, the venture did not materialize. Subsequently, Sumitomo decided to enter this field on its own. Other leading trading companies that have established their own supermarket chains include Mitsui, C. Itoh, and Marubeni Iida, three leading trading firms in Japan. While none of these firms has yet firmly established itself in this field, given their resources, they have great potentials for developing into major national chains. In addition, several leading trading companies are now planning to develop and manage shopping centers. Typically, to manage their retail operations, trading firms have organized separate subsidiaries, a pattern that they traditionally have followed in entering new fields.

Closely related to the foregoing is the entry of several major trading firms into the leasing of fully equipped supermarkets. Under this arrangement trading companies not only will construct store buildings but also will equip them and lease the fully equipped stores ready for operation. If desired by the lessee, the trading companies will also provide consulting service in designing the store layout, organization, and operations. Moreover, the lessee can obtain preferential treatment from the trading company if he wishes to purchase merchandise from it. This approach enables the trading company to enter into this field without having to assume day-to-day operating responsibility.

In addition to the income obtained from leasing, these trading companies hope that through the leasing relationship they can increase their sales of merchandise to supermarkets. Mitsui Bussan has been the leader in this practice. It established a separate department specializing in leasing activities for supermarkets in 1967, and by 1969 had entered into agreements with some 20 supermarket chains, one of which was Seiyu, the second-largest chain in Japan. For the fiscal year 1968 the contract with the Seiyu chain alone amounted to over ¥500 million.

Another significant step that major trading firms have taken so far is to strengthen their ties with existing large retail chains. Most notable in this approach is the 1969 agreement between Seiyu and the Mitsubishi Trading Company described in Chapter 3. The funds provided by the trading company will be used primarily to finance Seiyu's ambitious expansion program. What is most significant about this agreement is that it has gone considerably beyond what is considered a normal commercial relationship. A joint committee has been established consisting of managers at the operating level of both companies to coordinate the implementation of the agreements. The committee is charged with the responsibilities of coordinating production, processing, logistics, merchandise development, and import of foreign products.

This announcement was followed by other similar agreements. Even Daiei, Japan's leading supermarket chain, has entered a cooperative agreement with three large trading firms—Toyo Menka, C. Itoh, and Marubeni Iida. The agreement entered between Daiei and Toyo Menka, for example, is also quite broad in its scope. It stipulates, among other things: (1) that Toyo Menka will assist Daiei in its expansion efforts, including store leasing and marketing research; (2) that Toyo Menka will find foreign sources of merchandise; (3) that the two will cooperate in developing private brand merchandise for Daiei; and (4) that Daiei will increase its purchases from Toyo Menka.

Trading companies have also served as a link in creating formal cooperative relationships between major manufacturers and large supermarket chains. For example, in 1969 the Mitsubishi Trading Company was instrumental in linking Teijin Ltd., a major manufacturer of synthetic fibers, and Seiyu. Teijin will supply textiles to the Mitsubishi Trading Company, which, in turn, will convert them to finished ready-to-wear merchandise through their controlled subcontractors. The finished products will then be retailed by Seiyu. The three companies will also cooperate in developing original merchandise for Seiyu, and in this venture it is expected that the Mitsubishi Trading Company will play the chief coordinating role. A similar arrangement has been worked out among Toyo Rayon, Marubeni Iida, and Daiei.

Other firms have followed suit. In the fall of 1969, C. Itoh entered into an agreement to supply ready-to-wear merchandise to three major mass merchandising chains. What is significant in this arrangement is that the trading company and the three chains will cooperate in every stage of production, including deciding what and how much to produce. Actual manufacturing is performed by a network of C. Itoh's controlled manufacturers.

Similarly, major trading companies are now attempting to develop new channels of distribution for certain types of fresh food, such as produce, eggs, meat, and fish, specifically for mass merchandising firms. Trading companies are now attempting to cast themselves in the role of rationalizing outdated channels of distribution for these products and developing more direct and efficient ones to assure supply of a large quantity of standard-quality merchandise to major chains.

As a step toward this end, some trading companies have entered joint ventures with large chains to establish vertically integrated supply sources for meat, from cattle or hog raising to prepackaging. Mitsubishi Shoji established an egg farm that plans to supply fresh eggs directly to chains. Thus trading companies now have begun to mobilize their organizational skills to create new channels of distribution for a variety of products to meet the growing demand of the chains. This is particularly apparent in such fields as apparel and fresh foods, in which the traditional channels, dominated by a myriad of small production units, are inadequate to fill the need of the large chains.

In order to serve the needs of large retail chains better, trading companies have initiated other changes. These include establishment of a special organizational unit within the corporate structure to serve as the liaison between the company and the chains. They are also constructing merchandising and distribution centers to service chain accounts and are organizing special subsidiaries to supply only large-scale chains.

In addition to strengthening their ties with large supermarket chains, leading trading companies are also actively promoting organization of voluntary chains through their network of controlled wholesalers. The wholesalers, with assistance and guidance from trading companies, will organize their retail outlets into voluntary chains to which the trading companies will supply merchandise.

Other related activities by trading companies include entry into the distribution service field. Some trading companies, notably Mitsubishi Trading Company, have established a joint venture with Goldbond Stamp Company of the United States to sell trading stamps to retail outlets. Another major area of activities undertaken by leading trading companies is the development of shopping centers. Mitsubishi Shoji has entered into cooperative arrangements with a leading department store and two large mass merchandising chains to develop shopping centers. Mitsui Bussan has announced plans to build three large shopping centers in the Toyko metropolitan area. The management of these trading companies feels that in the development of shopping centers it can effectively mobilize and combine a wide range of resources, including financial power, organizational skills, and the support of their related firms.

There are several reasons why the alliance between major trading companies and large supermarket chains is mutually attractive. From the point of view of the trading companies, this constitutes a relatively painless way of establishing direct linkage with the mass consumer market. Trading companies will have ready, if not captive, outlets for some of the more important merchandise they handle. The arrangement will also make it possible for the trading companies to bring to bear, in a most effective manner, their advantages in the area of financial and managerial resources and well-established supply connections.

To supermarket chains, the alliance offers several advantages as well, not the least of which is access to the enormous capital resources that large trading companies have at their command. This will help finance their ambitious expansion programs, which, as we have seen, will require considerable amounts of capital. Moreover, these alliances assure the source of supply for two major lines of merchandise, food (fresh food in particular) and apparel. In soft goods, the manufacturing process goes through a series of stages, and trading companies are intricately involved in almost every stage. Their role is particularly important in converting textiles into ready-to-wear products. This process typically is performed by a large number of small establishments, and trading companies still maintain a firm control over them. Since soft goods have occupied a large share of the sales of mass merchandising firms in Japan, having dependable sources of supplies is extremely important.

With the growing size and number of supermarkets, the task has become increasingly difficult. Supermarkets have been confronted with a choice of undertaking their own manufacturing, either through their own facilities or controlled subcontractors, or relying on trading companies with already established networks of manufacturers. To supermarket chains, the choice was an obvious one, since undertaking their own manufacturing would make further demands on their already strained managerial and financial resources. Moreover, the alliance with trading companies would be helpful in developing their own private-brand merchandise. In fact, a number of original products already have been developed jointly and are being sold under existing brand names.

A similar situation is found for certain food items that are manufactured by a large number of small firms under the control of major trading companies. Moreover, with increasing volume, large-scale supermarket chains would need a more rational and efficient distribution system for food, including extensive development of frozen food and cold storage facilities. Here, too, the cooperation and assistance of trading companies could provide large chains with a ready-made source of supply. The closer relationships now evolving between large trading companies and large-scale supermarket chains have far-reaching implications.

Thus leading trading companies are making aggressive efforts to adapt their policies, strategies, and organizations to capitalize on the newly created opportunities in the mass consumer market. Of all the widely varied activities now being pursued by trading companies, particularly important has been their entry into the mass merchandising field—marking a new milestone for them. It is interesting, however, that trading companies were not an initiating force in promoting the growth of large-scale retailing. They entered this field only after its initial success had been all but proven.

Major trading companies have been making increasing efforts to find a niche in the mass merchandising field. As we have seen, they have much to offer to large chains, particularly in terms of financial and managerial resources and ability to provide an extensive network of procurement sources. Indeed, establishing close ties with mass merchandising firms offers promising potential to trading companies. To exploit these opportunities fully, however, there are a number of major problems to be overcome. Let us briefly consider the important ones.

MAJOR PROBLEMS OF TRADING COMPANIES

It is becoming increasingly clear that, to operate successfully in the mass merchandising field, trading companies must learn a great deal about retailing.

Second, dealing with the independent-minded and highly practical management of mass merchandising firms poses a difficult problem for the management of major trading firms. Simply entering into a cooperative relationship in procurement, merchandise development, or store leasing does not always make the collaborating mass merchandising firms captive markets for their products. On the contrary, the pragmatic managers of these chains, anxious to maintain their independence and eager to maximize their unique competitive position, are trying to keep the relationship as fluid as possible. Taking advantage of the eagerness of trading companies to enter this field, large chains often pit one against another to obtain better terms. Further complicating the relationship is the difference that exists in the orientation and attitudes of the managers of trading companies and those of chains. The former are professional managers and are the product of the nation's leading educational institutions, and as a group they tend to fit the mold of the "organization man." On the other hand, as we have already seen, the owners and managers of mass merchandising firms are highly individualistic, independent, self-made entrepreneurs with highly diverse backgrounds. In any case, although they see mutual advantages in collaboration, they are often suspicious of each other.

Finally, there is also some difference as to how each party perceives the emerging relationship. Trading companies naturally view the emerging cooperative relationship in store leasing, merchandise procurement, and so on, as a wedge to establish themselves in the mass merchandising field. On the other hand, mass merchandising firms assign to this relationship a much narrower role. To them it is only a means of achieving specific objectives, such as access to greater financial resources or dependable supplies of large quantities of standard quality merchandise. This difference is quite understandable. The relationship as of now is highly fluid, and there is every reason to believe that it will continue that way. Each party is feeling its way. Only out of groping experiments and through constantly changing power relationships will the future pattern emerge.

Whether or not leading trading companies can make significant impact in the mass merchandising field still remains to be seen. There is considerable controversy as to the eventual role of trading companies in this field. Some predict that large trading companies, with their tremendous resources, will emerge as a dominant force even in this area. Some assign them a more limited role.

OTHER PROBLEMS OF TRADING COMPANIES

Major trading companies are recognized as unique business entities throughout the world. In recent years, they have come a long way from institutions engaged only in commodity trading. They are highly diversified conglomerates whose business activities range from ocean development and mining to the fashion business. Only a decade ago, there was a widespread view in Japan that the role of the trading company was declining because of significant changes in the business environment. Instead, major trading companies have adapted themselves remarkably to such changes. Indeed, the resurgence of trading companies is fascinating. As successful and outstanding as the performances of the leading companies have been, they are not without problems and limitations. American business executives interested in dealing with trading companies are well advised to be aware of them.

Trading companies are vulnerable in several areas. First, in the marketing field, their experience has been largely in the area of basic commodities, and not with technically oriented products. By their very nature, trading companies are not well suited to market technically complex items. Thus, manufacturers of some of the more attractive growth products such as electronics, precision instruments, automobiles, or heavy machinery are undertaking many of their own domestic as well as international marketing activities. The phenomenal success of Sony in the world market, for example, has been achieved without the assistance of trading companies. Its success has been attributed almost entirely to its own sales efforts. Automobile manufacturers, notably Toyota and Nissan, are engaged in direct marketing efforts themselves in all the major markets of the world and are using trading companies only in small markets. Even when trading companies are used, manufacturers of technically oriented products find it necessary to provide strong technical support. As a result, trading companies are relegated to a secondary position.

A closely related, but a separate problem, is that as Japanese manufacturing firms gain experience in exporting, they need to rely less on the expertise of trading companies. The manufacturing companies are likely to terminate the relationship with trading companies or, short of that, will attempt to minimize their role.

Another problem is the lack of marketing skills, particularly in the field of consumer products. A number of American companies have found to their disappointment that trading companies cannot provide strong sales assistance. This, of course, is partly due to the very wide range of merchandise they carry, which often fragments their efforts. But more importantly, despite the trading companies' enormous experience in trading, they are weak in marketing knowhow, particularly in the consumer field. This deficiency is being partially corrected by the growing interest of trading companies in retail merchandising. But even here the results, as we have seen, are mixed. Management of mass merchandising firms that have dealt with trading companies are quick to point to the trading companies' relative lack of sophistication in consumer marketing.

The third problem is the change in the domestic distribution system. As examined earlier, the Japanese marketing system is now undergoing dynamic changes—changes in the direction of eliminating intermediaries. Large manufacturers have used trading companies as a primary marketing intermediary, not because of the marketing functions they can perform, but because of their roles in financing and as risk absorbers. But, it is by no means certain that the manufacturers will expect the trading companies to perform the same services in the future. The pressures for relationships with the distribution structure are now compelling the manufacturers to evaluate their traditional distribution practices, and the trading company's position is far from certain.

Fourth, the cozy relationship once enjoyed between the large city banks and major trading companies is undergoing some changes.

For a variety of reasons, the influence of major city banks is gradually eroding and they are now becoming increasingly aggressive in the search for their own clients, even including small to medium-sized firms. Contributing to the changing relationship is the trading company's growing interest in entering into factoring and leasing businesses—in effect, taking over some of the more lucrative business from the banks. This provides all the more reason for banks to decrease their alliance with trading companies.

Up until now, the single most important attraction of the trading companies to large as well as small manufacturers has been their financial muscle. The banks' increasing willingness to extend loans directly to manufacturing firms to meet their financing needs is likely to decrease their dependence on trading companies. The powerful networks of suppliers and customers of trading companies glued together by the financial capacities of trading companies may gradually disintegrate, depriving trading companies of an important competitive advantage.

The last, but not the least, problem faced by trading companies is the increasing diversification and complexity of their business and the diminishing ability of the management to deal with it. There are several closely related elements in this problem. First, the activities of trading companies are becoming so complex and diverse that they are now approaching a stage where they need to define what their business ought to be. Up until now, new functions have been added without their having a clearly defined set of criteria, guidelines, and policies. The trading companies have responded vigorously to growth fields as the opportunities arose. In fact, the entrepreneurial spirit present in large Japanese trading companies is striking, and has been looked upon by other industries with considerable envy. The management of trading companies has relentlessly searched for new opportunities and has been very successful in finding them. Many of their past diversification efforts, however, have been undertaken without central planning and coordination, and without explicit guidance from top management. An important question they now must face is whether or not they will be able to continue achieving the same feats.

The second element is also in the area of management. Trading companies are now confronted with the need to evolve a management system that is appropriate to their diversity and size. They must develop management skills which are quite different from those required by the traditional pattern, which was primarily geared to commodity trading. Whether or not trading companies are capable of developing management skills, systems, and organizations that are viable under these circumstances will pose a major challenge to their future.

Particularly difficult will be the transformation of the management mentality and outlook. The major thrust of trading companies until recently was in trading; thus, the management orientation and expertise, particularly of senior management, have been confined to that area. Now, recent developments have thrust them into the role of managers of large and complex conglomerates. The future of trading companies depends to an important degree on how effectively they can meet these challenges.

CHAPTER

6

STRATEGY GUIDE TO
THE JAPANESE MARKET

In this chapter we shall consider how American firms can penetrate the Japanese market. Specifically, we shall consider four key elements: (1) export strategy, (2) joint venture strategy, (3) negotiation strategy, and (4) strategy for dealing with the government.

EXPORTING TO JAPAN

Exporting to Japan by American firms has been growing at a steady rate during the past several years. Particularly, exporting represents an excellent way for small to medium-sized American firms to reach the Japanese market. In recent years, Japan's attractiveness as an export market has been increasing rapidly for several reasons. Notably, the Japanese government has been relaxing her once highly restrictive posture toward importing of foreign products. Foreign, particularly American, products in certain lines, still hold considerable appeal for the average Japanese consumer, and this is a distinct advantage to American manufacturers. Moreover, given the rapid increase in the income level, there is a steady trend toward trading up of consumers' purchase patterns, and products made in the United States are ideally suited for such a purpose.

Exporting offers several advantages to American firms as a means to reach the Japanese market. First, exporting can be achieved with a minimum commitment of resources. Second, exporting lends itself well to testing the market with a minimum of risk, and also to experimenting with various marketing strategies, product designs, and product mixes. Third, exporting makes it possible to prepare a way for undertaking manufacturing in a foreign country. Many successful foreign companies have built their market in Japan through exporting before they undertook local manufacturing.

How to Penetrate the Market

How can American firms penetrate the Japanese market successfully by means of exporting? The following guidelines have emerged out of a series of discussions with executives of American firms that have been able successfully to export to Japan.

1. <u>Know the market</u>. While this statement is so fundamental and obvious that it hardly needs special mention, this is one of the essential steps toward successful exporting. Surprisingly, however, some American firms began to export to Japan with only limited knowledge of the market; this has led to some grave consequences. In fact, a number of the firms studied began their exporting to Japan quite by accident. They began by responding to inquiries from Japanese agents, trading companies, or American distributors exporting to Japan. These companies typically viewed export to Japan as a marginal activity and responded to the inquires only on an ad hoc basis.

However, it is highly advisable to know the market at the very beginning. Now, a considerable amount of data is readily available about the Japanese market from a variety of sources, including the U.S. Department of Commerce, the Japanese External Trade Organization (JETRO), the Japanese embassy, and Japanese consulates located in major United States cities. These data are quite inexpensive and they are helpful in giving the interested company a rough estimate of the market. It is extremely important not to make any commitment without first getting some working notion of the potential size of the Japanese market for the product under consideration.

2. <u>Formulate a set of specific objectives</u> for your export operation to Japan. The objectives and targets must be realistic, consistent with the company's own resources. It would be helpful to have long-term as well as immediate objectives defined for the company's operations. The establishment of clear-cut long-term goals and strategies will go a long way toward preventing management from making an irrevocable commitment which may bind the company for many years to come.

3. <u>Know the government regulations</u>. While tariff and other import restrictions have been greatly liberalized during the past several years, there are a myriad of other government regulations which affect exporting to Japan. These regulations range from customs procedures, to laws governing specific industries such as foods and drugs, to those concerning Fair Trade. It is well to remember, too, that given the growing consumerism, enforcement of these regulations is becoming increasingly more strict.

4. <u>Analyze marketing tasks carefully</u>. It behooves every exporter to analyze what kinds of marketing tasks must be performed

by distributors, wholesalers, and retailers to sell the particular product effectively in Japan. Some of the relevant questions to be asked in this regard include: Is it a product new to Japan which will require considerable development efforts? How can these tasks be best performed? Who is in the best position to perform these tasks? How much technical support will be required? How about after-sale services?

A careful analysis of marketing tasks will be extremely important, and naturally this must be done in the Japanese context. Here, however, experience in the United States may be of considerable help, particularly for consumer products, since in many respects the Japanese pattern appears to follow the American development rather closely. Careful analysis of marketing tasks helps in the selection of agents in Japan, assists in negotiations with them, and aids in identification of the type of support needed.

5. <u>Support your exporting operations</u>. According to the American executives interviewed in this study, a common error committed by American exporters to Japan was their failure to support the export operation, once they entered into an agreement with a distributor. Somehow, the task became relegated to the distributor and the exporter expected the distributor to perform all the marketing functions. If the exporter's objective is very limited, or if for some reason the exporter is totally incapable of making further commitment, such an approach may be unavoidable. However, such neglect often takes place by sheer default. A foreign distributor, even more than a domestic one, needs support and assistance. American marketing experience may be helpful.

It is also essential to undertake periodic review of the distributor's performance. If the exporter has provided adequate support, such performance review can be done much more effectively. Providing support to distributors is a valuable means of communication with the distributor. In exporting operations, particularly to Japan, establishing an effective line of communication with the distributor is extremely difficult. Thus, providing support on a regular basis may go a long way toward building a favorable relationship.

6. <u>Keep abreast of new developments in the marketplace</u>. The Japanese market is very dynamic. It is going through rather volatile stages of development and information easily becomes outdated. When the economy sustains an annual growth rate of 10 percent or more, it can have a powerful impact on all segments of the society, including changes in consumer purchasing power, tastes, and even on the market structure. With improved purchasing power, new market opportunities are likely to open up and new segments may develop. It is not difficult to imagine the kinds of strains traditional marketing intermediaries were subjected to, when the output of and demand for the

products they were handling increased manyfold within a very short period of time.

If the American company is interested in continuing to tap the Japanese market, it will be extremely important to keep watchful eyes on the current development of the market and marketing practices.

It should be recognized that the Japanese market is extremely competitive. Japanese firms are particularly aggressive competitors, preoccupied with increasing their market share, and obsessed with an increase in sales volume. They may well resort to a drastic strategy to gain even a temporary advantage. Thus, if the exporter is interested in long-term development of the Japanese market, he should certainly keep close watch over major developments in that market.

How to Select a Distributor

In the foregoing, we have presented six major points to guide export operations. It would also be appropriate to consider what criteria to use in selecting a distributor—probably a trading company, since the overwhelming majority of American enterprises interested in exporting are using, or at least have considered using, trading companies. We have examined in an earlier chapter the very critical role played by trading companies in the Japanese marketing system. Thus, wise selection of a trading company by an American exporter is indeed an important key to success. Following are guidelines for choosing a trading company to market your company's products in Japan.

1. Evaluate carefully strengths and limitations of a specific trading company from the viewpoint of a given product or industry. Overall criteria such as general reputation and size of a firm are a good starting point, but should certainly not be the sole consideration. The general trading companies carry very broad lines of merchandise and each product division enjoys a considerable degree of autonomy. It is well to examine the strengths of each firm in the light of a specific line of merchandise.

2. Consider the attractiveness of a particular trading company from the standpoint of your firm's own objectives. Here, the definition of your company's objectives is the first essential task, followed by the analysis of the tasks required for successful marketing of the product under consideration.

3. Investigate the trading company's competence in consumer marketing. It should be remembered that the chief strength of the traditional trading companies lies in the area of basic commodities. Trading companies are relatively weak in the area of consumer marketing, particularly in market research and advertising.

4. Evaluate the executives who are directly responsible for your particular line of products. As noted earlier, the capability of a given trading company varies widely among product lines, and often the key consideration here is the caliber and experience of the individual or group of individuals who will be responsible for your particular line of products. If at all possible, identify the specific individual or group who will be in charge of particular product lines at the early stage of negotiations. You should also be aware that there are regular rotations of personnel in all major trading companies.

5. Find out beforehand what competing products the trading company handles. Trading companies do not generally enter into exclusive agreements. Thus, it is safe to assume that they carry competing lines of products.

6. Investigate ties with other Japanese firms. It is important to recognize that when an American company enters an agreement with one trading company, it will often be automatically thrust into an existing web of corporate ties with other Japanese companies. They include banks, manufacturing firms, wholesalers, and distributors. Such associations or affiliations could be a great asset, but it could also limit your firm's freedom and flexibility of action. This makes it critically important for you to assess a particular trading company in its totality, including its relationship with other firms.

JOINT VENTURES

Joint ventures with Japanese partners offer substantial benefits for foreign entrepreneurs considering entry into the Japanese market. But there are also potential pitfalls involved in this operation. Thus, it is critical for American firms to understand how to structure joint ventures. Though by no means exhaustive, the following guidelines are offered to persons contemplating such a venture in Japan.

1. Identify the objectives for the joint venture. Many joint ventures have been entered on the basis of vague goals with little effort being made to identify explicitly the objectives of the partners involved. Consider the following example. A well-known American manufacturer of consumer convenience goods entered a joint venture with a leading Japanese firm. Soon after the venture got underway, there developed serious conflicts of interest between the partners. After considerable probing, it became increasingly obvious that the original expectations of the partners were quite different. It was learned that the main motive for the Japanese company was to gain access to a particular type of technology developed by the American firm. Initially, the Japanese firm preferred licensing because it appeared to be the more flexible and least expensive way to achieve

its objective. The American firm, on the other hand, was anxious to establish a base of operations in the rapidly growing Japanese market and insisted on direct investment. The American firm attached considerable importance to the joint venture as a vehicle for future expansion in Japan. In contrast, the Japanese partner viewed it merely as a glorified licensing agreement. This difference in basic objectives and motives was glossed over in the pre-entry planning and negotiation stage in a facade of goodwill. Needless to say, the goodwill faded rapidly and the outcome was disappointing for both partners.

Differences in the basic objectives of a venture frequently go undetected until it gets well underway. When the differences are discovered, they are so basic that compromise is impossible and the partners then reach an impasse, with disastrous results. The first and most urgent task for the American enterprise interested in forming a joint venture with a Japanese firm is to identify its own set of objectives as clearly as possible (surprisingly, this is often not done) and to seek to understand the motives of the prospective Japanese partner.

2. Anticipate major sources of differences and reach explicit understanding prior to the formation of the joint venture. In the planning stage, it is important to anticipate possible areas of conflict. Some of the problems to be faced by American joint ventures in Japan are no different from those arising in international joint ventures elsewhere. These include understanding about disposition of earnings, division of export markets, determination of transfer prices, and the conditions under which new products and technology are made available to the joint venture.

3. Obtain and evaluate sound data on the Japanese market. The prospective U.S. partner must undertake a thorough investigation of the investment climate and market conditions on his own. This third guideline may be obvious to most readers, but it is not always practiced by American executives interested in establishing joint ventures in Japan. Too frequently the American entrepreneur relies on the data provided by the prospective joint venture partner, sometimes supplemented by superficial statistics available in the English language. Then, he may not make a thorough and rigorous evaluation of the data.

Particularly important is the accurate assessment of market potentials. Understanding the market places the American firm in a better bargaining position. Moreover, the very process of investigating may well lead to the identification of new opportunities, heretofore undetected. In this investigation, the collection of quantitative data is important, but the gathering of qualitative information is equally important. In fact, the latter is essential in assisting American management to interpret properly the quantitative data. Collecting such qualitative information should certainly include visits to retail or wholesale outlets and to typical urban and rural households.

4. Evaluate your prospective partner carefully. The importance of careful assessment of a prospective partner cannot be overemphasized. In evaluating a prospective Japanese partner, a proper framework is necessary. Financial statements alone tell little about a company. In-depth information, much of which is qualitative in character, must be carefully collected and assessed.

Of particular importance is the prospective company's relationship with other companies. In Japan there are a number of powerful enterprise groups of various types, the most powerful based on former Zaibatsu ties. The contemporary Zaibatsu group is basically different from the prewar version as there is no central holding company. Nonetheless, intercorporate ties among member companies can still be strong. Mitsubishi, Mitsui, and similar groups are quite formidable. Mitsubishi, the largest and most influential Zaibatsu group today, does considerable business within the group, which consists of nearly thirty major corporations, including a bank and a trading company. It is estimated that roughly 30 percent of the combined sales of the Mitsubishi group are made within the group.

Aside from the Zaibatsu groups, there are other groupings based on trading companies and banks. While these groups are much more fluid and the degree of intragroup loyalty is not nearly as strong as in the case of the Zaibatsu groups, still it is an important factor. In entering a joint venture with a given Japanese firm, the American company may well be taking on a relationship with a host of other corporations as well. The group affiliation may be an asset for the venture, giving it ready access to other group companies, but it may well exclude the new venture from certain valuable segments of the market.

5. Be aware of Japanese personnel policies. Another important, but often little understood, aspect are the personnel practices of the prospective joint venture partner. The so-called permanent employment process and seniority-oriented personnel customs are perhaps the two best known aspects of Japanese managerial policies. A Japanese firm assumes responsibility for its employees for their entire career. Moreover, appropriate positions must be assigned commensurate with age.

This practice, among other things, necessitates shifting less capable individuals out of the mainstream of corporate activities. A common custom has been to transfer these men to subsidiaries, affiliates or subcontractors. Such transfers occur most frequently in the few years before they reach the compulsory retirement age. Not infrequently. Japanese companies have used the newly created joint ventures as a haven for persons who have not been promoted to top management positions. A few enlightened Japanese firms, recognizing potential problems of such a personnel practice, have a policy of using joint ventures as a training ground for promising young executives. The prospective partner's personnel practices deserve careful consideration.

HOW TO NEGOTIATE IN JAPAN

Many American executives have found it exceedingly difficult to conduct negotiations with Japanese executives. The language difficulties are formidable enough, but in addition there are some fundamental cultural differences which make communication difficult. Effective communication, of course, is the first step toward successful negotiation. American executives find that the peculiar Japanese manner of decision making is difficult to understand. In the course of this study, the author has made an intensive investigation of the process of negotiation between American and Japanese executives and out of this experience the following guidelines have emerged.

1. Prepare adequately before you begin negotiations. The importance of adequate preparation cannot be overemphasized. It will mean getting basic data on Japan, the Japanese economy, the peculiarities of a given industry, and recent business and technical developments that are relevant to your industry. Particularly important, of course, is thorough understanding of the Japanese economy. Many materials on Japan are now available in the English language. Thus it is possible to gain an adequate understanding of Japan, which will place you in an excellent position for negotiation, give you flexibility, and open new options. You should recognize that your Japanese counterpart is likely to have considerable knowledge about your company, industry, and relevant recent developments in the United States. It is important that you begin your negotiations on an equal footing.

2. Identify your objectives clearly before you begin negotiations. Surprisingly, it has been found that American executives do not always enter negotiations with a set of well-defined objectives. Moreover, it is critically important that the negotiating team on the spot and the home office or corporate headquarters be in complete agreement on the objectives. The U.S. company's position should be clearly established and communicated to the negotiating team, which then should be given a considerable degree of flexibility. In the negotiations the Japanese counterparts will have ready and immediate access to their top management, if the need should arise. This is especially true if the meetings are held in Japan. If the representatives of the American companies must consult with their home

office on every detail they will be saddled with a serious handicap. Moreover, it is extremely important for the corporate headquarters to support the negotiating team by speedily responding to the team's requests for data, opinions, and information.

3. Prepare your presentation well. The manner in which the negotiating teams carry on the negotiations reflects on the general reputation of the company. The Japanese will watch you closely and with discerning eyes. This is particularly important if the American company is smaller and less well known than the Japanese counterpart. An excellent, well-prepared presentation will go a long way toward successful negotiations. It is vital that your presentation is concise, logical, and clear. You should not expect your interpreter to clarify your points.

4. Accept the fact that the decision-making process in Japan is time consuming. The Japanese decision-making process can be characterized as group-oriented-consensus. In the process, the U.S. negotiators may well find it necessary to spend a considerable amount of time with lower-ranking Japanese managers. You should recognize that in Japanese negotiations lesser members of the Japanese team, regardless of their position, often play a much more important role than their status might indicate. A common mistake made by American executives, particularly senior executives, is their insistence on talking only with their counterparts. This may be necessary and desirable for reasons of protocol, but it is often dangerous to insist on this blindly. An important aspect of the Japanese style of decision making is that although the process is slow, once the decision is made, implementation usually proceeds speedily.

5. Recognize that decision making is a continuing process. You should establish and maintain effective channels of communication with your counterpart so that you will know how negotiations are progressing. Don't simply wait for a reply, but monitor the reactions of various individuals as the proposal is circulated and considered by different groups within the corporation.

6. Be flexible and subtle. The Japanese do not appreciate blunt and bold use of power. Do not hold rigid positions if you can avoid them. Do not issue ultimatums. Be sensitive to subtle clues and hints.

7. If you find it necessary to break off your negotiations, do so gracefully. Many American managers have lived to regret having terminated negotiations too abruptly. Remember that the Japanese business community is a closed system with an intricate network of communication, cutting across companies, even industries. The manner in which you terminate your negotiations with a particular company may well determine your success with another firm.

HOW TO DEAL WITH THE GOVERNMENT

One of the recurring problems faced by American executives in doing business in Japan is their relationship with the Japanese government. Throughout this study, those American executives interviewed confirmed once again the critical nature of this aspect of doing business in Japan. Although restrictions on importing and capital entry have been significantly liberalized during the past several years, the government still exerts considerable influence on the private sector. Indeed, it behooves every American businessman interested in business relations with Japan to be familiar with the role of the government in the conduct of business, and develop an understanding of how to deal with it.

In this section we shall briefly examine the nature of the business and government relationship in Japan. First, government influence is pervasive in the conduct of business, but Japan is by no means a planned economy. Public ownership is extremely limited. Since the early days of the nation's industrialization, business activity has been largely in the private sector; however, in recent times the government has maintained a close relationship with the business community.

Second, the Japanese view of what the role of government should be is based on an entirely different premise than in the United States. It would be a serious error to view business-government relationship with a culturally bound view. The manner in which the government and business interact reflects the cultural heritage of the nation. What makes the business-government relationship distinctive is the style with which the interactions take place. The relationship is less legal, more informal. There are few formally regulated industries in Japan. This informal nature of interaction is mystifying and perplexing to American businessmen.

Third, while the government plays a vital role, there is great danger in exaggerating its role, power and influence. Its influence is pervasive but not all-encompassing, and is not always accepted. The government-business relationship has not always been smooth. There are some instances in which the usually effective consultative and cooperative approach has not been effective. Japanese bureaucrats are highly pragmatic and they are prepared to back down from their position whenever they feel that the cost of enforcing their guidelines is prohibitively high. The label, "Japan, Inc.," is a gross oversimplification of the process of interaction. When the government is said to play an all-powerful directive role this is a misinterpretation of the business and government relationship. The relationship is much more consultive, coordinating, and cooperative.

Fourth, despite the outward appearances to the contrary, it must be noted that the Japanese government is by no means a monolithic or cohesive entity. There are inter-Ministry rivalries, differences of view, and power struggles. It is dangerous to assume that the Japanese government always speaks with one voice. Finally, it is vitally important to be aware that Japanese government influence varies considerably among industries and even within a given industry over a period of time.

Against the foregoing background, the following guidelines have been prepared for American businessmen dealing with the Japanese government.

1. Recognize that government influence is pervasive and that the style of dealing with the government is different from the practices prevailing in the United States. Avoid attaching a value judgment to the Japanese pattern of interaction. Such preconceived notions seriously curtail one's effectiveness.

2. Be aware that the Japanese bureaucracy is divided clearly into two tiers for career advancement: (a) a small number of the very elite career bureaucrats who follow well-planned and prescribed career paths, and (b) the great majority whose advancement opportunities are severely limited. The very elite group are most capable and highly qualified. Persons with whom American executives will be dealing are of the highest caliber. It is well to recognize, however, that procedural and routine matters are handled by the second group of bureaucrats who possess a great deal of expertise in a narrow field and who are in a position to exert considerable influence in processing relatively routine matters.

3. Accept the Japanese style of decision making. In the Japanese bureaucracy, as in most corporations, the decision-making process stresses the consensus approach. Lower ranking officials tend to have much greater influence than their formal status might suggest. It is critically important, then, for American executives to be sensitive to this pattern of decision making.

4. Recognize that Japanese government officials are likely to have different customs and criteria for their decision making than those to which U.S. businessmen are accustomed. This is understandable, and it must be accepted. It is important to cultivate channels of communication with the relevant officials. Informal exchange of views is extremely important. Contrary to a notion widely accepted by U.S. businessmen new to the international scene, more experienced American executives in Japan have found that the Japanese bureaucrats, given their excellent ability and qualifications, are often much more flexible and open to new ideas than the inexperienced group assumes.

5. Consider the government-business relationship as a continuing and long range one. Nourish your government contacts. It is also advisable to keep the relevant Japanese Ministries abreast of your plans.

6. Do not leave the government relationship entirely in the hands of your Japanese partner or lawyers. Government relations should be a key top management function. No doubt, your Japanese partner can perform many of the day-to-day governmental contacts, but it is vitally important for American executives to be involved directly with key negotiators within the government. Government relations are far too important to leave solely in the hands of a law firm or partner, however capable.

We have briefly presented practical guidelines for those who would penetrate the Japanese market. This market is expected to show continuous growth. Moreover, the operating climate in Japan for foreign firms has become quite favorable since the latest round of capital liberalization, which went into effect on May 1, 1973. While highly competitive, Japan still offers one of the most exciting growth markets in the world.

ABOUT THE AUTHOR

M. Y. YOSHINO is Visiting Professor at Harvard Graduate School of Business Administration. He has served as a consultant to the McKinsey Co. and the Ford Foundation.

He is the author of Japan's Managerial System: Tradition and Innovation (Cambridge, MIT Press, 1968) and The Japanese Marketing System: Adaptation and Innovation (Cambridge, MIT Press, 1971), as well as numerous articles on international business.

Dr. Yoshino received his Ph.D. from Stanford University in 1962.

RELATED TITLES
Published by
Praeger Special Studies

JAPANESE PRIVATE ECONOMIC DIPLOMACY:
An Analysis of Business-Government Linkages
William E. Bryant

TRAINING JAPANESE MANAGERS
Allen Dickerman

MARKETING IN THE SOVIET UNION
Thomas V. Greer

JAPAN: FINANCIAL MARKETS AND THE
WORLD ECONOMY
Wilbur F. Monroe
foreword by Edwin O. Reischauer